# Beyond

*Exploring th*
*everyday English*

## Clandon French

ISBN: 9798769727061

Copyright © 2021 Clandon French.

Book design by Peter Small.

Front cover art © Ray_of_Light/Shutterstock.com.

Published by Clandon French.

## Authors

Gillian Boreham, Michael Cutler, Daphne Davidson Kelly,
Jenny Frendo, Maria Grasso, Graham Moore,
Marie-Jo Morelle, Gill Saunders, Peter Small, David Turnbull,
Gay Umney

**Coordinator:** Marie-Jo Morelle

# Table of Contents

# About this book

Do the French still recognise the French words we use every day and do they have the same meaning and pronunciation in modern day French? In this engaging book Clandon French has chosen a selection of French words which are used in English and researched their origins – how and why they came to be used in English today. Broken down into ten subject areas, this book will fascinate and inform all those who are interested in the evolution of language.

The ten subject areas are: Law and legal matters, Food and Gastronomy, Cinema, Art, Politics, Music, Sport and Games, Travel and Tourism, Fashion, and Literature and Drama. Each is covered in a separate chapter.

# Introduction

*Marie-Jo Morelle*

## The Genesis of this book

The authors of this book are members of an advanced French
language class that has been meeting weekly in Clandon.
Through discourse with our teacher, who is French by birth
and nationality, it became apparent that the language phrases
we explored in articles from the written media and news in various forms (radio, television, songs, poetry, literature, art, films,
humoristic cartoons...) all conveyed more than the meaning of
their bare translation. Repeatedly we stumbled over the hidden
knowledge present in the expressions or words chosen to communicate ideas. Roland Barthes's book on mythology and semi-
ology (Barthes 1957) came to mind; especially his illustration
on how a word or an expression, within one same linguistic loc-

# Introduction

ation, can be interpreted in many different ways depending on the context and on the acquired knowledge of the speaker/ reader or listener.

In observing the language used in the French media, Barthes concluded that social, psychological and cultural backgrounds will all have a significant impact on how one perceives the world within one's own language. Does it mean that it is impossible to understand fully 'the mysterious boundaries' present in a language? Probably not, but it requires a long journey into the cultural traditions, ways of life, historical events and traumas that have marked our mutual collective unconsciousness.

In our group, we all understand French well enough to be able to grasp the nuances that sometimes need 'unpicking' to get to the root of an idea or concept. The foreign perception of the British way of life of our teacher, a French native speaker, has helped guide us to another level of understanding within all the above considerations. This has generated numerous fascinating discussions on selected topics in particular, and on life in general.

## The trauma of Brexit and of the lockdowns

The departure of the UK from the EU, Brexit, forced us to review our attachment to common European values. It was then that we discussed the use of French words and expressions in the English language. We all had laughed at the use or misuse of English words in French texts (*le parking/le week-end/le business/le cluster/débreaker/liker/le cocooning* ....) while there were equivalences. We mostly agreed that as English, the lingua franca, was predominant in the world, it was therefore inevitable for English and American words to make their way into the French language if only to reflect the globalisation of trade and culture. Yet, our teacher quizzed us on the reasons of using French words and expressions in the English language of today.

A quick look in Wikipedia reveals an extensive list that lacks both humour and humanity. To our knowledge there is today no interesting publication on the subject.

Of course there are obviously historical and cultural reasons behind this permanent or fleeting 'borrowing' which would be interesting to unpick.

We already know that numerous scientists have tried to explain how social creatures great and small acquire language within the process of life itself.

In French, there is a fundamental difference between *langue* and *langage* as discussed by de Saussure (1967). In his *Cours Linguistique Générale*, he argues that *langue* is what an individual internalised without awareness and passively, as language is an individual use of *langue* ('speech'), which requires an intellectual effort.

Foucault (2008) introduced furthermore the concept of *discours* or discourse, which added a political and ideological dimension linked to power and truth. Although no one has found a universal, easy to understand explanation on how exactly language evolves, most agree that without social interactions, life would not be as we know it. It is therefore widely

# Introduction

accepted that linguistic interactions are at the heart of the awareness of the self and of the world at large, including others. In spite of the famous quotation of Jean-Paul Sartre (1994), '*L'enfer, c'est les autres*' (Hell is other people), how could one aspire to a world without others? Could one enjoy the Garden of Eden in a solitary state?

Sharing is part of the joys of life, as we have now all realised only too well through the current 2020 and 2021 national or local lockdown situations. We have rediscovered that the art of communication, the sharing of ideas and the enjoyment of acquiring knowledge using our creative minds, is a recipe for a fulfilled life. Zoom became our virtual meeting place and a space for making sense in French of what was happening.

It is only via good, reliable communication and the production of great ideas that mankind is able to improve its chances of survival, improve its quality of life, travel in space, and think the unthinkable. The Covid vaccine is one irrefutable example of this process. So too is the speed at which everyone, young and less young, embraced and understood the available technology of Zoom/Skype/Teams/WhatsApp, etc. at our micro level in order to continue communicating and interacting.

Our now virtual Clandon French is privileged to be thinking right now the unthinkable! We want to be creative as well as entertaining to our potential readers with a book exploring some French words and expressions that have slipped into the English language. Our challenge is to unpick the palatable roots for this intrusion. This collaborative and collective / publication is a 'lockdown' attempt to find out why and how, unknown to most French people, so many French expressions have been adopted by the English language.

## A quantum approach

Like Wittgenstein (2014), one could argue that language can unlock private life and so becomes the key to helping us to know ourselves. It is a fact that, if a lion could speak we would not understand each other, each of us coming from different thought processes and idiolect that drive our totally different lives. Luckily, our two nations, UK and France, share enough common history and traumas to understand one another to a certain extent. Yet, there are huge gaps.

Since discourse and language in all their manifestations help us to make sense of, or at least come to terms with, our seemingly chaotic and illogical reality, we have adopted a thematic approach and have organised the content of the borrowed 'words and expressions' in selected topics reflecting the interests of the co-writers. Our main group interests are food and gastronomy, travel and tourism, fashion, politics, art and literature, sport and music, and finally cinema. Because creative and visual art, literature and poetry help us not only to frame our perception of the world but also, though the power of dreams, give us the ability to change it, we explore the changes associated with the identified French substitutes in a friendly, innovative, poetic, individual and literary way as it suits the author of each chapter.

Of course, discourse and languages furthermore belong to an order of knowledge and cannot be isolated from its attached

# Introduction

ideological foundation (Foucault 2008). We therefore include our observations and analyses, when appropriate, on this acquisition of language/ knowledge not as continuous, but as it comes in small but discrete historical, political or social units.

In addition, since language and linguistic skills become tools to achieve not only the sharing of ideas and culture, but are also a form of empowerment, we provide our own analyses and explanation on how the acquisition of French expressions can occur both as static facts and like waves of ideas (fashion, leisure) thereby demonstrating the acquisition as a dynamic process. In fact, some expressions will lose their pertinence as others will appear in the process of the evolution of knowledge as illustrated by expressions such as *art nouveau, mise en scène* and *cinéma d'auteur*. It is also physically impossible to isolate a unit of acquired language from its living context. The more precisely something is defined, the more at risk it is of becoming irrelevant or obsolete.

There will always be a difference between the world of languages and reality as both occur in an unpredictable manner. So we accept the possibility of making historical errors, misrepresentations and wrong interpretations.

# Introduction

## References

Barthes, R. (1957) *Mythologies*. Paris: Éditions du Seuil.

Foucault, M. (2008) *L'archéologie du savoir*. Paris: Éditions Gallimard.

Sartre, J-P. (1994) *Huis-clos*. Éditions Gallimard.

de Saussure, F. (1967) *Cours de Linguistiques Générales*. Paris: Éditions Payot.

Wittgenstein, L. (2014) *Philosophical Investigations*. 4th ed. Edited by P. Hacker and J. Schulte. Chichester, England: Wiley-Blackwell.

# Beyond the Words

# 1 – Law and Legal Matters

*Daphne Davidson Kelly*

## Influence of French, particularly Norman French, on the English Legal System

The conquest of England in 1066 by William the Conqueror, Duke of Normandy (or as some like to call him 'William the Batard') heralded a change in language with the introduction, or the imposition, of Norman French into the English language. One of its products was 'law French', a mixture of French, Latin and Anglo Saxon used in the Law Courts.

The unsuccessful Revolt in 1076 by the Anglo Saxon Earls was a rebellion by three earls led by Roger de Breteuil against William. This was the last serious act of resistance against William and resulted in William imposing stricter laws in order to strengthen his hold over Anglo Saxon England, which included

# 1 – Law and Legal Matters

ending the use of Anglo Saxon legal terms and the compulsory use of French terms, or law French, in the Law Courts. The earliest known documents in which French (i.e. Anglo Norman) is used for commentary on English law date from the third quarter of the 13th century and include two particular documents:

1.  The first is *The Provisions of Oxford* (1258), consisting of the terms of oaths sworn by the 24 magnates appointed to rectify abuses in the administration of King Henry III, together with summaries of their rulings.
2.  The second is *The Casus Placitorum* (c.1250–c. 1270), a collection of legal maxims, rules and brief narratives of cases.


During the 14th century, vernacular French suffered a rapid decline. The use of law French was criticized by those who argued that lawyers sought to restrict entry into the legal profession.

The Pleading in English Act 1362 ('Statute of Pleading') acknowledged this change by ordaining that thenceforward all court pleading must be in English so 'every Man....may the better govern himself without offending of the Law'. From that time, law French lost most of its status as a spoken language having become *trop desconue*. It remained in use for the 'readings' (lectures) and 'moots'. In many cases the French words came to mean something entirely different to their original meaning.

# 1 – Law and Legal Matters

In 1399 a text recorded in French and Latin, *The Record and Process of the Renunciation and Deposition of Richard II*, and the rolls of parliament, were used to support Henry IV's statement of claim to the throne and the apparently willing relinquishment of the Crown by the deposed Richard II ('with cheerful countenance' he signed the Declaration). An English translation of the document was used. Henry IV was the first English king since the Norman conquest (Reign 1399–1413). This would further establish the use of English in legal and parliamentary writings. The dictionary of legal terms, *Termes de la Lay*, translated into English in 1527, set the meaning and definition of legal expressions and showed an active law French vocabulary of less than 1,000 words. Legal writers had begun to insert English words in substitution. Language changes quickly to suit its purpose and its use.

By the age of Elizabeth I a French visitor to England would hardly recognise many of the French words used, so much had their meaning been adapted as well as the pronunciation changed, and gradually over time law French terms were anglicised. Under the rule of Oliver Cromwell (from 1653), with its emphasis on removing the relics of archaic ritual from legal and governmental processes, a further blow was struck at foreign languages and in particular French legal terms. Even before then, in 1628, Sir Edward Coke acknowledged in his preface to the *First Part of the Institutes of the Law of England* that law French had almost ceased to be a spoken tongue. It was still used for case reports and legal textbooks until almost the end of the century, but only in an anglicized form.

# 1 – Law and Legal Matters

If there were any obstacles to changing from law French, it was that it was felt that law was scarcely expressible in English. As in present day law, there is a reluctance to change or modernise arising from a fear of losing the true meaning or nuances of terms, and so create ambiguity where tried and tested terms had succeeded in the past. Gradually English replaced French as the legal language, but law French wouldn't die easily and some words still exist. Although law French as a narrative legal language is obsolete, many individual law French terms continue to be used by lawyers and judges in common law jurisdictions.

Among these are the following few examples:

### *Assizes*

*Etymology*

From Old French *assise,* past participle of *asseoir*: to seat – which came to mean sittings or sessions of judges on legal actions.

*History*

Originally the Courts were peripatetic, travelling from one part of England and Wales to another on commissions of *oyer and terminer*: to hear and determine – and courts were set up and juries summoned in the various assize towns. From 1293 sets of judges toured four circuits and from 1328 six circuits. The sitting or sessions of judges were known as 'justices of assize'. In 1956 Crown Courts were set up in Liverpool and Manchester replacing assizes and quarter sessions. In 1972 following a report by a Royal Commission civil matters were referred to the

High Court and criminal matters to the Crown Court and the judges no longer moved from town to town.

*The word is still in use – in Scrabble!*

### *Chose*

*Etymology*

From French word *chose*: a thing.

*History*

In law this refers to property or things and is applied to personal property, as in 'choses in possession', which are personal things of which one has possession. It also refers to 'choses in action', which are situations where the owner of the thing has not the possession but a right of action for their possession. Examples are rights to receive or recover a debt or damages for breach of contract but which cannot be enforced without an action, hence teamed with 'action'.

*You just have to take care if you chose a chose in action!*

### *Defendant*

*Etymology*

From French *défendant*.

*History and meaning*

The party against whom a legal proceeding is taken.

# 1 – Law and Legal Matters

## *Jury*

### *Etymology*

From Anglo Norman *juré* meaning 'sworn', an 'oath' or 'inquiry'. Also from Latin *jurare*: to swear.

### *History*

A jury is a sworn (*juré*) body of people (the jurors) convened to render an impartial verdict (a finding of fact on a question) officially submitted to them by a court, or to set a penalty or judgment. Juries developed in England during the Middle Ages, and are a hallmark of the Anglo-Saxon common law legal system. They are still commonly used today in the United Kingdom, the United States, Canada, Australia, and other countries whose legal systems are descended from England's legal traditions.

Most trial juries are 'petit juries', and usually consist of twelve people. A larger jury, known as a grand jury, was used to investigate potential crimes and render indictments against suspects, but all common law countries except the United States and Liberia have phased these out. The modern criminal court jury arrangement has evolved from the medieval juries in England. Members were supposed to inform themselves of crimes and then of the details of the crimes. Their function was therefore closer to that of a grand jury than that of a jury in a trial.

Juries are most common in common law adversarial system jurisdictions. In the modern system juries act as 'triers of fact' while judges act as 'triers of law'.

# 1 – Law and Legal Matters

## *Judge*

*Etymology*

As with most words the origin is Latin *Jus* and *Judex*, and so to old French *Juge*. Juxtaposed with the Latin *dicere* the concept of 'Judiciary' arises. Also 'Judgeman' – which became 'judgement' – which came to mean the declaration of the law by someone who declares the law.

*History*

More generally the word is used for a person who evaluates something and forms an opinion or applies the rules.

## *La reine le vault*

*Etymology*

From French *la reine le veut*: The Queen wishes it.

*History*

This is a Norman French phrase used in Parliament even today in the UK or England anyway to signify that a public Bill has received royal assent from the monarch, whether in reality she likes it or not – like the Prorogation Bill of 2020.

## *Parole*

*Etymology*

From Old French *parabola – parole*: word.

# 1 – Law and Legal Matters

*History*

The word now has a further meaning of a formal promise from ecclesiastical *parabola*. This becomes 'word of honour' especially by a prisoner of war, who would give his word not to escape if allowed to go about at liberty. In modern days it is the undertaking or promise of a prisoner on conditional release from jail not to breach certain conditions placed on his liberty.

## Tenure

*Etymology*

From Old French *tenir*: to hold, and from Latin *tenere*: to hold.

*History*

In the 15th century it meant 'holding of a tenement', from Anglo-French and Old French where tenure meant 'a tenure or estate in land'. The sense of 'condition or fact of holding a status, position, or occupation' is first attested in the 1590s when it became the idea of a 'guaranteed tenure of office' usually at a university or school. The root also extends to 'tenants' who are renters or leaseholders i.e. 'holders' of some interest in land.

*You could say: the tenacious tenant tenanted his land!*

## Oyez

*Etymology*

Originally Latin *audire* then French/ Old French *oiez* dating from about the 15th century, taken from Anglo-French *oyez* 'hear ye'!

# 1 – Law and Legal Matters

*History*

It was a cry uttered, usually three times, and was a call for silence and attention. In the early 15th century it was a shout for silence before a proclamation made by an officer of a law court. Street criers used this as well – loudly shouting 'Oyez Oyez Oyez' while ringing a hand bell before distributing some evening news, or news not yet in paper form, and free from the press barons.

*So no fake news in those days!*

## Prochain ami

*Etymology*

Possibly Latin in origin *prope*: next. Then both a French and Anglo-Norman term and both words still in current use. In old law this was *procliein ami, prochein cousin* or *prochein ami* meaning 'next friend'. Similar to 'next of kin'.

*History*

As neither a woman or an infant could legally sue in her or his own name, any action had to be brought by her or his *prochein ami* or now *prochain ami*; that is, some friend (not being a guardian) who will appear as plaintiff in her or his name. The prochain ami could also in this capacity bind an infant as an apprentice where there was no legal guardian. It was not always litigious.

In 1870 the Married Women's Act gave women in some cases the right to own their (own) property. In 1882 an Act established for the first time the separate legal personhood of women – meaning they could sue and be sued in their own name.

*Sadly then there are no more prochains amis for women in those cases!*

The term Next Friend is now used in English Law as a 'litigation friend' and is someone accompanying a person under questioning by the police or some other investigating authority. This equally translates to the term Mackenzie Friend – which is a phrase used to describe someone not necessarily legally trained who acts as an adviser or counsellor to a plaintiff or defender undertaking his or her own suit in court. The Mackenzie Friend advises and does not actively participate. The Friend can now charge fees in England but not in Scotland but in neither country is the Friend protected by legal indemnity insurance.

Also interesting perhaps to note is *Prochein avoidance* in this case translates as 'Next vacancy', which is a power to appoint a minister to a church when it shall next become vacant.

### *Profits à prendre*

*Etymology*

Profits: originally Latin *profectus*: advance growth increase. Also *proficio*: to go forward, advance, make progress.

*History*

This is a right to take something from another person's land. This could be part of the land itself, such as peat; something growing on it, such as timber or grass (which can be taken by the grazing of animals); or wildlife killed on it, for example by shooting or fishing. The thing taken must be capable of owner-ship, so a right to use land in some way, or to take water from a natural feature, cannot be a profit. Today it would be relevant in the right to graze on common land.

Rights of common for the purposes of the Commons Registration Act 1965 are likely to be one of the following:

- Rights of pasture (including cattle-gates or beast-gates – rights to pasture a specified number of animals).
- Rights of pannage (to turn out pigs to eat acorns).
- Rights of turbary (turf cutting).
- Rights of estover (to collect wood).
- Rights of piscary (fishing).
- Rights of common in the soil (to take stone, gravel).

These rights can still be registered with the Land Registry.

*All these profits are for the taking!*

### *Tort*

*Etymology*

From French *tort* meaning a wrong, injustice or crime, in turn from Latin *tortus* meaning 'twisted'.

*History*

In law this is the legal concept of a wrongful act or an omission or an infringement of a right (other than under contract) or a breach of duty leading to a legal liability. 'Tort' gives rise to injury or harm to another and amounts to a civil wrong for which courts impose liability. In the context of torts 'injury' is the invasion of any legal right whereas 'harm' describes a loss or detriment in fact that an individual suffers. Public nuisance is a crime as well as a tort.

There are seven recognised international torts – akin to the seven deadly sins. Four of these are criminal: assault, battery, false imprisonment and intentional infliction of emotional distress. The other three are civil: trespass to chattels, property, and conversion. The main difference between 'trespass to chattels' and 'conversion' is the degree of interference. 'Conversion' occurs when a person uses or alters a piece of personal property belonging to someone else without the owner's consent.

*The law of tort can be justifiably described as tortuous!*

### *En ventre de sa mère*

*Etymology*

From French meaning literally 'in the mother's stomach' or an unborn child. This was until very recently used in Will writing where the children or grandchildren or remoter issue of the Testator were to have rights of succession. The phrase covers children who were not born as at the date of the Testator's death. So if conceived as at the date of the Testator's death and born alive thereafter they would fall in line to equal succession with their peers.

*History*

Nowadays, with the move towards transparency and simplification of language in law, there is a tendency not to use the term.

However, it is understood as a legal principle and unborn children (that is, in foetal form at the date of the death of the Testator) will have rights to succession, unless excluded.

## Conclusion

I have chosen only the above few words and phrases as these are recognised today as French words by Francophones although their meaning, and in some cases pronunciation, has been changed from the pure French or the equivalent word found today.

These words and phrases have their roots in the French language (as with most romance languages deriving from Latin or Indo-European) and were imported into English at the time of the Conquest.

With the decline of the Norman occupation, its influence, by way of the vocabulary, changed and grew to reflect the idiolect and phonetics of the indigenous population. Language grows according to use and thought and philosophy, and the methods of expression.

Language and the law are always problematic. Legislation, by way of statute or case law, is an indication of what is right and what is wrong, and the words used to define concepts are not amended without lengthy consideration. This leads to texts and laws and precedents that are frozen in the vocabulary of their time. Conversely language never freezes. It is constantly being redefined and readjusted in the light of present day conventions and mores, and to suit new circumstances and new ideas. It changes, it adapts, and new meanings are given while older meanings are lost entirely.

Law French is a perfect example of how language can be considered at one time so exact and so appropriate in its context and yet within a couple of hundred years its vocabulary becomes a mystery.

## References

This chapter uses material from the following Wikipedia articles, which are released under the <https://creativecommons.org/licenses/by-sa/3.0/> Creative Commons Attribution-Share-Alike License 3.0.

<https://en.wikipedia.org/wiki/Law_French/>

<https://en.wikipedia.org/wiki/Jury>

<https://en.wikipedia.org/wiki/Assizes>

<https://en.wikipedia.org/wiki/Chose>

[Accessed 10 November 2021].

# 2 – Food and Gastronomy

*David Turnbull*

France and Great Britain are two countries separated by a narrow strip of water. They have far more in common than most people imagine: art, cinema, football, rugby and a sense of humour based on the absurd all spring to mind. However, *pétanque*, cricket and each other's languages still cause total bafflement and confusion. The purpose of this chapter is to examine the influence of French language and culture on British gastronomy.

We need to distinguish between cooking and gastronomy. British cooking is excellent and has largely remained unchanged for hundreds, indeed in some cases nearly a thousand years. It comprises three cooking styles: boiling or steaming; roasting or baking; and frying. Ingredients are generally standard also: farmyard animals, fish and vegetables. Until recently the latter were brought home from greengrocers or market stalls in brown paper bags and had to have the mud washed off to see what they were. Sadly, see-through plastic has ended this lucky dip. These are all accompanied by untold numbers of glass bottles and jars containing a vast array of pickles, chutneys, *condiments*, *sauces*, flavourings, jams and other preserves.

British cooking has survived not because of a statutory body set up to ensure its survival but because it has remained nutritious, tasty, well prepared and affordable. Any day of the week at about 5 o'clock Fish and Chip shops in just about every town in the land open up. Their customers know what they will get and what it should taste like. Similarly, pubs with signs chalked on a board outside offering 'Sunday Roasts' welcome guests with remarkably similar fare. Even the banter between customers, staff and proprietors is predictable. There is no reason why such food will not remain unchanged for another millennium, long after foams, spherification – a culinary process that employs sodium alginate and either calcium chloride or calcium glucate lactate to shape a liquid into squishy spheres, which visually and texturally resemble roe – and the use of liquid nitrogen have accompanied each other onto the scrap heap of culinary history.

Although British cooking has remained unchanged it is not as prevalent as it was. There has been a huge parallel growth in the food of other countries: Italian, Thai, Indian, Greek, Chinese, Bangladeshi and Turkish are among the most popular. The greatest foreign influence however has been from the French who have developed and retained a reputation for high quality and inventiveness.

French influence on British food has been very much driven by the untimely deaths of monarchs or other heads of state. The first of these to go was King Harold II of England with an arrow in his eye. The victorious Normans brought their style of cooking with them and insisted that the new servant class of Anglo Saxons learnt the French vocabulary of *boeuf*, *porc* and *mouton* for their favourite meats. These now anglicised words would not today be recognised in France although the term *rosbifs* is slang for British tourists and reflects the colour they turn after a few hours in the sun.

The proximity of England and France meant that there were always exchanges of one sort or another between the two countries. Intermarriage between the various royal families remained popular and Calais was an English parliamentary constituency until 1558. However, there were no great gastronomic changes until 1649 when King Charles I had his rather severe haircut.

The Establishment of the Commonwealth by the parliamentarians after the death of Charles I led to an exodus of British nobility to France. They returned from 1660 onwards, many with much more developed tastes than before they left. They also came back with the very first recipe books, which demonstrated the French move towards more complex dishes with a great attention to detail.

When products and ideas have come from overseas the English have always found it easier just to use the accompanying foreign word rather than go to the lengths of inventing a new English one. This is especially true in the case of gastronomy where great chunks of the French dictionary have been assimilated unchanged.

At around this time societal differences also began to affect eating habits in the two countries. English nobles generally only visited London as and when necessary. They were more than happy to return to their country seats to manage their estates and to dine and socialise with their neighbours. New-fangled ideas about cooking therefore remained in London and traditional, local, cooking styles continued (Irish Stew, Lancashire Hotpot, etc.).

In France on the other hand everything circled around the court either in Paris or, later, Versailles. Noblemen dreaded being away from court and often returned to find themselves side-lined. This concentration of money and power in a small area saw the development of what has become *haute cuisine*. New ideas included new techniques of cooking (*sauté, brulé*), much lighter dishes and more modest presentation of individual dishes.

The next significant death was in 1793 when the French decided to follow the English practice of decapitating monarchs, in this case Louis XVI. The subsequent wars did little to affect the British attitudes towards French cooking as many escaping French chefs sought employment in Britain. Indeed, any animosity between these chefs and their new employers was frequently the other way round. Marie-Antoine Carême was Chef de cuisine to the Prince Regent but disliked everything about England and the English and preferred to try his luck in revolutionary France rather than stay another minute with us. The Duke of Wellington's chef was so disappointed with the reception his food received he left, reportedly saying 'If he were a hundred times a hero, I could not serve such a master and pre-serve my powers; my body might live but my genius would die' (Dickson Wright 2012). After the revolution *sauces* such as *velouté* and *béchamel* began to be developed. The rescue of highly concentrated and tasty residues from the bottom of cooking vessels, *déglacé* was an essential part of concentrating flavour. The English generally still preferred traditional gravy which prompted Voltaire to declare, '*il y a en Angleterre soix-ante sectes religieuses différentes, et une seule sauce*' (there are 60 different religious sects in England and just one sauce).

Probably the most influential French chef to arrive on these shores was George Auguste Escoffier who came to the Savoy hotel in 1890. His belief that *haute cuisine* should be kept simple has had a lasting impact on the popularity of French cuisine. Although he left England under a cloud of suspected financial irregularity, his name is immortalised in the slang term 'scoff' for a good meal.

A few years later in 1914 the assassination of Archduke Franz Ferdinand set off half a century of catastrophic events in Europe and millions of British soldiers went to fight in France and neighbouring countries, many gaining their first experience of foreign food, which they were surprised to find they liked. Although the slaughter of young servicemen in the Great War was never repeated, the death of Paul von Hindenburg from lung cancer in 1934 led indirectly to the unleashing of an unprecedented degree of carnage and terror across Europe.

# 2 – Food and Gastronomy

During this period and probably for twenty years after 1945 many French chefs ended up in Britain often marrying girls from areas far from London. There are numerous tales of small towns and villages hosting a family-run, chequered table-clothed restaurant serving simple food brilliantly cooked. Competing restaurants opened by the British often over-promoted themselves pushing their *Cordon Bleu* (whatever that means) credentials to the extent that Gordon Blue became a derogatory term for anyone pumping out small portions of badly cooked overpriced stuff that people neither recognised nor liked.

The use of French culinary terms has always been extensive and widely understood. Their use does not usually signify any sort of pretence but does demonstrate the remarkable flexibility of the English language. As well as the words introduced above, methods of cooking and presentation include *blanché, en croute, en papillote, frappé, gratiné, sous-vide,* these processes often involve things like a *bain-marie* or a *bouquet garni.* Food preparation and service also has its own vocabulary. I have discovered eight terms for cutting up potatoes and root vegetables but baton and julienne are probably the best known. Even in non-French establishments the order of the courses is usually expressed using some or all of the following: *amuse bouche, hors d'oeuvre, entrée* and *dégustation*.

The phrase '*oui chef*' is bandied around continually on cookery programmes. There is no easy translation of this, the best I can come up with is 'Go away you pompous over-promoted oaf. Shut up. I know what I am doing and it will be ready when I say it is'.

The assumption in any country that foreigners trying to speak one's language are idiots and unable to be understood applies to food as well. When hotels still had telephonists a request by a Brit in a Paris hotel to be connected to his parent company in Los Angeles led to his call being transferred to the kitchen for them to cook his requested dish of *l'os en gelé*.

No discussion of the assimilation of French words into the English language would be complete without a quick look at *faux amis*. For example, words whose roots are in France but which the French themselves would not recognise include jelly, scoff, beef, pork and Gordon Blue. The British also use words they think are French but which have different meanings when translated back: preservative (or *preservatif*), legumes, raisin, éclair, Marmite and serviette. Other mangled words such as French Fries, French Dressing and *Crème Anglaise* do not fit in any of the above categories and seem a good point at which to stop.

## Reference

Dickson Wright, C. (2012) *A History of English food*. London: Arrow Books.

# 2 – Food and Gastronomy

# 3 - Cinema

*Maria Grasso*

Cinema, described as *le septième art,* is an artistic term used to describe the genre of film; film making, the film industry and to the art form that is a result of it. To confirm its historic roots, near the Parc Butte-Chaumont in Paris is the road Cours du Septième-Arts in the 19th arrondissement. Thanks to the Lumière Brothers, who in 1885 experimenting with photographic plates had invented a new 'dry plate' process of developing film. They were able to generate enough money to open a factory in the suburbs of Lyon and worked on a way to project the film onto screen so that many people could view it all at the same time. They came up with a device called the *cinématographe*, a three-in-one device that could record, develop and project motion pictures becoming the first viable film camera. *La Sortie des ouvriers de l'usine Lumière* is considered the first motion picture. In 1896 various theatres opened up in London, Brussels and New York with 40 films and documentaries following that same year. After black and white film came colour in 1918, followed by the 'talking pictures' 12 years later.

In the 1950s, the French 'New wave' (*Nouvelle Vague*) emerged as a new movement. It was characterized by its rejection of traditional film-making conventions in favour of experimentation. It is perhaps considered as one of the most influential movements in the history of cinema.

The 'New Wave' film-makers explored new approaches to editing visual style and narrative, as well as engagement with the social and political upheavals of the era, often making use of irony or exploring existential themes. The term was coined by a group of French film critics and cinephiles associated with the magazine *Cahiers du cinéma*. These critics rejected the tradition of quality and the aesthetic of mainstream French cinema, which emphasized craft over innovation and old works over experimentation. This was apparent in a manifesto-like 1954 essay by François Truffaut, *Une certaine tendance du cinéma français*, where he denounced the adaptation of safe literary works into unimaginative films. Along with Truffaut, a number of writers for *Cahiers du cinéma* became leading 'New Wave' filmmakers, including Jean-Luc Godard, Éric Rohmer, Jacques Rivette, and Claude Chabrol. The associated Left Bank film community included directors such as Alain Resnais, Agnès Varda, and Chris Marker. Using portable equipment and requiring little or no set-up, film-making often presented a documentary style. The films exhibited direct sounds on film stock that required less light. Filming techniques included fragmented editing and long takes. The combination of realism and subjectivity created a narrative ambiguity in the sense that questions that arise in a film are not always answered in the end. Leaving the viewer to make their own conclusions. In 1950 *Les Enfants Terribles* (literally meaning 'naughty children') created by Jean Cocteau and Jean-Pierre Melville who were young, passionate and brilliant film directors also created *The Strange Ones*, a surrealist film for its time. The novelist Raoul Mille declared: 'All these directors of the new wave are more men of letters than film-makers because they speak the language of writers' (Prédal 2005). These writers and directors, innovative and unorthodox in their style, touched on subjects such as homosexuality, incest and sadomasochism. A stark contrast to the mainstream cinema of the time, this proved to be another form of Nouvelle Vague.

Financially French cinema is the third largest in Europe and Cannes holds one of the most important international film festivals every year, previewing new films of all genres from around the world. The film industry has grown over the years, especially in Hollywood, California and Bollywood, India producing the largest number of films in the world.

Although cinema is a relatively new form of art, French influence is indisputable. It is therefore not surprising to find French cinematographic expressions in the English language as illustrated below.

## French cinematic terms used today

### *Film noir*

*Film noir* is a genre of film, literally meaning 'black film', a style characterized by cynical heroes together with the effects of austere lighting and often based on complex intriguing plots. It developed in the early 1940s and blossomed in the post-war era in American cinema. The French critic Nino Frank described the Hollywood films of 1946 as 'the crime dramas after World War II', which focused on oppressive atmospheres, menace, anxiety and suspicion. The subject matter was often bleak with a sombre, downbeat tone. The plot together with low-key lighting (harsh shadows and *chiaroscuro*) and often night scenes, depicted disillusioned and jaded characters, together with canted camera angles. The settings depicted a gloomy underworld of corruption and the iconography of guns and urban settings presented a dark atmosphere of pessimism, tension, cynicism and oppression. *Film noir* often portrayed crime subjects who were usually set in grim, seedy cities. Criminals, anti-heroes, private detectives and duplicitous femmes fatales would dominate its screens. In 1955 Henri-Georges Clouzot directed the film, *Les Diaboliques* a 'horror-film noir' in which the wife of a tyrannical headmaster at a boarding school and his mistress conspire to kill the scoundrel. The film creates an unbearable sense of dread and dark beauty.

### *Matinée*

In the 1930s–60s an afternoon spectacle also known as *matinée* was the afternoon movie. It was the precursor to the soap opera and the term 'matinée idol' referred to the male heart-throbs who acted in them.

### Cinéphile

Cinéphile refers to a devotee of films and is derived from the ancient Greek κῑνέω (*kīnéō*, 'to move'), *cine,* together with *philia* meaning 'love of' and describes someone who has a passion and interest in films, theory and film criticism. Originally it referred to a film-maker.

### Rôle

A *rôle* describes the part a character takes. It is played by the actor who pretends to be someone else. The word originates from the Latin 16th century *rotulus* and then *rota* or *roue* which are now obsolete. Then later came the roll of paper (*rouleau*) on which the actor's part was written.

### Montage

Montage is a creative film-editing technique in which a series of shots is sequenced to condense space, time and information. In the early 1900s it was a useful device for overcoming the drawbacks of the silent movies, which were labour intensive. The word derives from the French verb *monter* or *assembler.*

The most common definition of editing is Marcel Martin's 'the organization of the shots of a film in certain conditions of order and duration' (Prédal 2005). Opening up the possibilities of experimentation almost to infinity, it upsets aesthetic practices even in the spectator's perception of the film. It is thus more than a technique and no English word can better express what the word encapsulates.

The Soviet film *Battleship Potemkim* directed by Sergei Eisenstein in the 1920s first used this technique in which he interposed multiple shots with each other in a single scene. He created five methods: metric, rhythmic, tonal, over tonal and intellectual montage. Using the finest examples of montage, *Battleship Potemkim* is cited as one of the best propaganda films ever made, proving to be an emotive form of film-making.

## *Critique*

A critique is written by someone who views, takes notes and analyses the acting, plot development, writing, directing, editing and cinematography of a film. They use their writing and analytical skills to craft a professional review that can help audiences determine whether or not they should view that particular film. Academics or journalists will critique films for the benefit of an audience through newspapers and magazines. In French, the term is broader and includes all those who, in the media, make judgements about the works.

## *Farce*

This refers to a light-hearted, gleeful, often fast-paced and crudely humorous contrived and 'over the top' comedy that broadly satirizes, pokes fun, exaggerates or gleefully presents an unlikely or improbable situation (*comique de situation*); an example would be a tale of mistaken identity, cross-dressing as in the 1973 film *La Cage aux Folles*; directed by Jean Poiret it is considered a mainstream cult classic. Often characterized by pratfalls and other physical antics, most types of farces include screwball comedy, bedroom sex farce/comedy (*comédie de boulevard*), a contrast to parody and satire.

According to the Larousse dictionary, the genre of farce took shape in the 16th century in stories and comic dialogues. It described real-life situations that had something of a buffoonish quality.

In English, the meaning of farce is still understood today as improbable and unlikely staged situations full of physical antics including scenes of a sexual nature.

In French, a farce (a joke or a prank) is also an action intended to make someone laugh at the expense of someone else by means of mystification, prank, hoax and trick (*faire une farce à quelqu'un*).

### Dénouement

*Dénouement* is the French word for unknotting. Derived from the French *dénouement*, which literally means 'untying', taken from the Middle French *desnouement*, from *desnouer* (to untie), from the Old French *desnoer* and from the Latin *nodare*, *nodus* ('knot').

It was first used in 1705 to describe what expires after the climax of a narrative in which the complexities of the plot are unravelled and the conflict is finally resolved. In the denouement of a traditionally structured plot, the villain may be exposed, the mystery explained, a misunderstanding clarified, or lovers reunited. In a tragedy, the end is often called a 'catastrophy' (catastrophe). However it is important to point out that it is not the final conclusion but a plotted conflict's unfolding and resolution (Encyclopedia Universalis).

In modern French, on the other hand, the *dénouement* is only the way in which an action, a literary work, a film, etc., ends; an event that marks the end.

### Homage

An homage is a show of respect or dedication to artistic work in the film world. It is when the film-maker references or imitates another film-maker's work. This can be done visually (e.g. copying a movie scene's style or action) or audibly. Many film-makers pay homage to other films, as for example Quentin Tarantino in *Kill Bill* (2003) who replicated exact moments from *Citizen Kane* (1941), blending them together to create his own distinct vision.

In 2019, at the opening of the Cannes film festival, homage was paid to Agnes Varda for all her contributions to cinema. This confirms the difference in meaning between French and English homage.

In French, the meaning is more complex. The notion of imitation is excluded.

### Tour de force

A cinematic tour de force refers to an actor or writer who performs or achieves great skill in a film or performance. Someone who is incredibly skilful, brilliant, notable and reflects a very high standard.

# 3 - Cinema

## *Portmanteau*

A portmanteau refers to a film consisting of several shorter films, usually tied together by a central theme or idea or by a linking event. In French, *un portemanteau* (*un porte-manteau*) is a large suitcase. The word comes from French *porter* 'to carry' and *manteau* 'mantle', or 'cloak' – so it's what you carry your clothes in. A portmanteau (*un mot-valise*) is also a word made by combining two other words.

## *Première*

A *première* refers to a first public performance or showing of a film or play. Every year in Cannes the first official public screening of a movie, marks the kick-off or opening with a lavish international event; champagne flows and the red carpet comes out. First held in 1946 for the recognition of artistic achievement, the festival came to provide a rendezvous for those interested in the art and influence of the movies. It became an international marketplace where producers and distributors could exchange ideas, view films, and sign contracts. As an opportunity to celebrate the heritage of film and present new films and highlight works of the past, the *Festival de Cannes* has remained faithful to its founding purpose to draw attention to and raise the profile of films, with the aim of contributing towards the development of cinema, boosting the film industry worldwide and celebrating cinema at an international level.

## *Genre*

Originally a French word meaning 'kind', 'sort' or 'type'; it refers to a class or type of film (i.e. Westerns, sci-fi, etc.) that shares common, predictable or distinctive artistic and thematic elements or iconography (e.g. bad guys in Westerns wear black hats), narrative content, plot and subject matter, mood and milieu (or setting), or characters. Film genres are distinct from film styles (a recognizable group of conventions used by film-makers to add visual appeal, meaning or depth to their work).

### *Grand Guignol*

*Grand Guignol* literally means 'large puppet' in French, and originally refers to the famous classic shock Montmartre Parisian theatre (during the 1900s), which specialized in grue-some melodramas with gory special effects; the term now refers to a film or play with sensational, macabre, horrifying, dramatic and Gothic content. In 1935 *Mad Love*, directed by Karl Fre-und and based on Maurice Renard's novel *The Hands of Orlac*, this film is a perfect example of Grand Guignol theatre as a principal setting – the story of Gogol the doctor obsessed by the leading actress at the Theatre of Horrors. When her fiancé's hands are crushed, Gogol replaces them with the hands of a killer.

### *Pastiche*

A word to describe an artistic work that imitates another. The word pastiche is originally French, but borrowed from the Italian word *pasticcio*. It came about to celebrate great works of the past. It is a cinematic device honouring another film-maker's cinematography through imitation.

The black & white film *Les Tontons flingueurs* (1963) is a suc-cessful example of a stylish pastiche of film noir. A comedy by Georges Lautner (1926-2013), it is adapted from a thriller novel by Albert Simonin, starring famous French actors of the time including witty and self-deprecating dialogue (Hayward 2003).

## References

Encyclopædia Universalis, *Montage–CINÉMA.* Available at: https://www.universalis.fr/encyclopedie/cinema-realisation-d-un-film-montage/ [Accessed 10 November 2021].

Hayward, S. (2003) *Cinema studies*. London: Routledge.

Merriam-webster.com (2019), *Merriam-Webster Dictionary*. Available at: https://www.merriam-webster.com/dictionary [Accessed 10 November 2021].

Prédal, R. (2005) *50 ans de cinéma français (1945-1995).* Paris: Armand Colin.

Wikipedia, https://wikipedia.org.

# 3 - Cinema

# 4 - Art

*Gillian Boreham*

## Introduction

Since pre-history, through cave paintings and carvings on rock and bone, there is evidence that mark-making has been a powerful form of communication. Although art can be said to transcend the spoken language, being mainly an immediate form of communication without the need for words, it has inevitably collected its own language over many centuries, drawing from the roots of artistic movements, techniques and materials. France has always been rich in the field of art and it is inevitable that some of the art terms used in France have become embedded in the English language, adding richness and diversity to our own. Many artistic movements started in France before expanding to the wider world and we still recognise them by their original French terminology.

In the following pages some of these French usages are explored, not only for their linguistic value but also in celebration of the rich heritage of art influences over the centuries between France and the United Kingdom.

*Let's begin and it is all in the initials!*

*First take your pencil!*

Although the English word 'pencil' has moved on from its Anglo Norman roots, vestiges of its origin still exist today. The word 'pencil' comes from the Old French *pincel* from the Latin *pencillus*, or 'little tail'.

The modern pencil was invented in 1795 by Nicholas-Jacques Conté, who was a scientist serving in Napoléon Bonaparte's army. These early pencils were first made using pure carbon called graphite first discovered in Europe at the start of the 15th century although used by the Aztecs as a marker several hundred years earlier. Conté discovered that by using a clay binder and adjusting the ratio of graphite to clay, pencils enabling mark-making of varying softness and darkness could be produced. Today's pencils are graded according to the mix of clay and graphite giving a variation of line to accommodate varying uses and users. These are graded as: 2H, H, HB, 2B, 3B, 4B, 5B, 6B, 7B, 8B, 9B. Although there are some conflicting views, the H is believed to be for the French *Haut*, or high, while the B for the French *Bas* or low. The H denotes a higher quantity of binder to graphite giving a harder line, while the B signifies a lower quantity of binder creating a higher pigment deposit and a darker stroke.

*Now for colour!*

The French word *crayon* originally meaning 'chalk pencil' dates to around the 16th century and derives from the word *crate* (chalk), which comes from the Latin word *creta* (earth). The word crayon is now used in English to describe wax crayons.

*Now for the paper!*

The English word has moved away from the modern French *papier* but it shares its French roots. The word 'paper' comes from the Anglo Norman *papir* from the Latin *papyrus* or 'paper reed'. We do, however, still make use of the modern French *papier* to denote particular uses and techniques in art.

*Now some techniques and processes to try out!*

### *Papier Collé*

This French term translates as pasted paper and is a type of collaging technique in which paper is adhered to a flat mount; whereas collage may incorporate non-paper materials, papier collé refers only to the use of paper. The term papier collé is mainly used in reference to the paper collages of the Cubist movement. A notable example is George's Braque's *Fruit dish and glass* (1912). The cubist Georges Braque first used this technique when drawing on imitation wood-grain paper pasted onto white paper.

# 4 - Art

## *Papier-mâché*

This literally means 'chewed paper', 'mashed paper' or 'pulped paper'. It is a composite material consisting of paper pieces or pulp; this can be reinforced with textiles, bound with glue, starch, or wallpaper paste.

The technique originated in China, the inventors of paper itself, and was used to make items such as mirror cases, snuff boxes and warrior helmets dating back to about AD200 during the Han dynasty. Its use in Europe began in the 18th century, and by 1725 gilded papier-mâché was used as a cheaper alternative to plaster or carved wood. In Russia in the 19th century there was a thriving industry in the production of decorative items especially small boxes some of which were for sale in Tiffany's during this period.

Papier-mâché rose to popularity in Georgian and Victorian England between 1720 and 1900. The use of 'japanned' papiermâché became popular, imitating the lacquered wood of Japanese lacquered work but using papier-mâché in its place.

Furniture makers used papier-mâché mixed with tar or pitch enabling them to create a surface similar to polished black lacquer. These objects were usually very decorative, often incorporating shells, mother of pearl and gold decoration.

## *Collage*

This is another sticky process! This term for sticking or gluing describes both the technique and the work of art produced in which pieces of paper, fabric and other materials are stuck down onto a surface. Collage first began in China around

# 4 - Art

AD200 with the invention of paper. It was used in 10th century Japan when calligraphers applied glued paper, using texts on surfaces when writing poems. Collage was also used in Medieval Europe and by the 15th and 16th centuries the technique was used to apply gemstones and precious metals to religious artefacts and images, including icons. In 1912 Pablo Picasso and George Braque began using collage in their creative work. Today a new term 'ecollage' can be used for a collage using computer skills.

*Notable examples:*

3.  *Fruit dish and Glass* by George Braque, 1912. Papier Collé and charcoal on paper.
4.  *Compotier avec Fruits, Violin et Verre* by Pablo Picasso, 1912.
5.  *Au Vélodrome* by Jean Metziner, 1912.
6.  *Petit Déjeuner* by Juan Gris, 1914. Gouache, oil, crayon on cut-and-pasted printed paper on canvas.

### *Décollage*

This French word literally means 'to take of, or unstick' and is associated with a process used by artists of the Nouveau Réalisme group, an artistic movement founded in 1960 by the art critic Pierre Restany and the painter Yves Klein at their first collective exhibition at the Apollinaire Gallery in Milan. They proclaimed 'Nouveau Realisme - new ways of perceiving the real'.

## *Frottage*

Literally, French for 'rubbing'. This is the technique of obtaining an impression of a surface texture by placing paper over it and rubbing with a soft pencil, crayon or coloured wax. The finished result also has the term frottage. This technique was used by Max Ernst and other members of the surrealist movement. An example of this technique is the Max Ernst work *The Origin of the Clock*, from Natural history c1925 published 1926.

## *Pointillism*

What's the point? Pointillism is a technique of painting where the artist uses small dots of colour to form the painting rather than traditional methods of blending pigments on a palette. This technique was developed in 1886 and extended from the Impressionist style of painting. This method was originally developed by George Seurat and Paul Signac.

*Notable examples:*

1. *A Sunday afternoon on the island of La Grande Jatte* by George Seurat, 1886.
2. *L'Hirondelle Steamer on the Seine* by Paul Signac, 1901.
3. *Sailboats and Estuary* by Theo van Rysselberghe, 1887.
4. *La Recolte des Pommes* by Camille Pissarro, 1888.

## *Tableau*

This French word for painting is a descriptive term first used by the French philosopher and writer Denis Díderot in the *Entretiens sur le fils naturel*, 1757 and *Discours de la poésie dramatique*, 1758 in regard to compositions both on stage and in painting, constructed with figures to give the overall impression of being natural and true to life.

*Notable example:*

1.  *An experiment on a bird with an air pump* by Joseph Wright of Derby, 1768.

## *Pastiche*

This French word formed from the Italian *pasticcio* denotes a work of art that imitates the style or character of the work of one or more other artists. It celebrates rather than mocks the work it imitates.

*Notable examples*

The works of Mychael Barratt, e.g. Richmond Park, 2019.

## *Trompe-l'œil*

Literally, 'deceives the eye'. *Trompe l'œil* creates the illusion of the real on a flat surface. The artist tricks the viewer into seeing a two-dimensional surface as a three-dimensional space. Although the terminology originates with Louis-Léapold Boilly who used it as the title of a painting he exhibited in the Paris Salon of 1800, this illusionistic technique was often used in Greek and Roman murals.

Italian painters Andrea Mantegna (1431-1494) and Melozza da Flori (1438-1494) painted illusionistic ceiling paintings in fresco to give the impression of space to the viewer below. Many Italian painters came to use the technique often adding a small *trompe-l'œil* feature to their paintings. *Trompe-l'œil* painting became very popular in Flemish and Dutch painting in the 17th century, employing this technique in still life painting.

*Notable examples:*

1. Trompe d'œil Table top by Louis-Léopold Boilly, before 1793. National Trust Wimpole Hall.
2. An example of trompe l'œil can be seen at Chatsworth House in Derbyshire in a trompe l'œil painted around 1723.
3. The Painted Hall of the Old Naval College, Greenwich.
4. *Escaping criticism* by Pere Borrell de Caso, 1874.
5. *Still Life* by Samuel Dirksz Van Hoogstraten, 1664.

### En Plein Air

This means the act of painting outdoors.

In contrast to studio painting this approach enables the artist to better capture the changing details of weather and variations in light and colour. Before the 19th century painters had to mix their own paints from raw pigments, which made painting outside impractical. This changed in the 1800s owing to the introduction of ready-mixed tubes of paint enabling the artist to work freely outside. The Impressionists embraced this approach and the opportunities it provided to study the effects of light and atmosphere.

*Now some key movements in Art to explore!*

### *Impressionism*

Impressionism is the name of an artistic movement that started in Paris in the early 1860s when four young painters, Claude Monet, Pierre-August Renoir, Alfred Sisley and Frédérik Bazille met while studying under the academic artist Charles Gleyre. They shared their joint interest in painting in the open air directly from nature. Their aim was to reproduce an impression as it was experienced and without being constrained by generally recognised rules. They worked mainly outdoors *en plein air* aiming to capture changing effects of light and colour using separate fragmented brush strokes and pure colours

This artistic movement, which started in France, spread to other countries in the second half of the 19th century and the first quarter of the 20th century.

*Notable examples:*

1. *Paysage au bord du Lez* by Frédérik Bazille, 1870.
2. *Poppy Field* by Claude Monet, 1873.
3. *Gare St Lazare* by Claude Monet, 1877.
4. *Bridge at Villeneuve-la Garenne* by Alfred Sisley, 1872.
5. *Bar at the Follies-Bergère* by Eduard Manet, 1881.
6. *The Seine at Asnières* by Pierre-August Renoir, 1879.
7. *Summer* by Berthe Morisot, 1878.

# 4 - Art

## *Art Nouveau*

Literally means 'New Art'.

*Art Nouveau* is an international style of art, architecture and decorative applied art. The style is often inspired by natural forms and has a sense of dynamism and movement. There was an emphasis on breaking down old distinctions between fine and applied arts.

The first *Art Nouveau* houses were constructed in Brussels in the 1890s, of particular note being those designed by Victor Horta. The style moved to Paris and was adapted by Hector Guimard for the entrances to the new Paris Metro. It was at the 1900 Paris International Exposition that this movement introduced the work of *Art Nouveau* artists Louis Tiffany, René Lalique and Émile Gallé. The new movement was further influenced by the works of the Pre-Raphaelites and the Arts and Crafts movement in England.

*Notable examples:*

1. Paris Metro stations, e.g. Abbesses, designed by Hector Guimard.
2. Tiffany Glass.
3. La Maison Horta, Brussels (Musée Horta).

## *Avant-garde*

Literally, 'the advanced guard' or 'vanguard' being the part of the army that goes in advance of the rest.

# 4 - Art

It was Claude Henri de Rouvoy, Comte de Saint-Simon, a French political, economic and socialist theorist who first used the term *avant-garde* in regard to art and artists.

In his book *Opinions Littéraires, philosophique et industrielles* published after his death in 1825, he states, 'It is we artists who will serve you as the avant-garde... the power of the artists is in fact most immediate and most rapid: when we wish to spread ideas among men, we inscribe them on marble or on canvas.... What a magnificent destiny for the arts is that of exercising a positive power over society, a truly priestly function, and of marching forcefully in the vanguard of all the intellectual faculties'.

This term has come to be used to describe work that is experimental, radical or unorthodox and has been associated with movements in modern art where work is bold, innovative and progressive.

*Once your work is completed!*

### Oeuvre

Literally, 'work'. This French noun is used in English to describe a substantial body of work constituting the lifework of an artist.

*Then Exhibited!*

### Vernissage

The process of varnishing. *Vernissage* is the term used for the preview of an art exhibition, this may be private before the formal opening and limited to invited guests.

Originally in the 19th century before official exhibitions such as those at the Royal Academy, artists would put the finishing touches to their work by varnishing them prior to the formal opening of the exhibition. This has developed into the private views of today...

...and just may, in the future, form the whole, or part of, a *catalogue raisonné*.

## Catalogue Raisonné

French for 'reasoned catalogue'. A *catalogue raisonné* is a comprehensive, annotated listing of all the known works of an artist or group of artists, either in a particular medium or all media. It plays an important part in the authentication of an artistic work and may take many years of research in its compilation. It describes the work in a way that enables reliable identification and may be considered the supreme arbiter of the genuine and the fake.

Edmé-François Gersaint (1694–1750) compiled the first significant catalogue raisonné on the work of a single artist in Western Art history. This work, entitled *'Catalogue raisonné de toutes les pièces qui forment L'œuvre de Rembrandt'*, was published posthumously following his death in 1750 having been augmented by Helle and Glomy who published the work in 1751. An English translation appeared in London in 1752 as 'A Catalogue and description of the Etchings of Rembrandt Van-Rhyn, with some account of his life'.

# 4 - Art

## References

Diderot, D. (2005) *Entretiens sur le fils naturel*. Paris: Editions Flammarion.

Glorieux, G. (2002) *À l'enseigne de Gersaint*. Champ Vallon.

Jeremy Norman's Historyofinformation.com (2021) *Edmé-François Gersaint issues the first significant Catalogue Raisonné in Western Art History, on Rembrant's prints*. Available at: <https://www.historyofinformation.com/index.php#entry_1761> [Accessed 10 November 2021].

Katz, R. and Dars, C. (1994) *The Impressionists handbook : the greatest works and the world that inspired them*. Southampton: Colour Library Direct.

Michel, P. (2008) *Le commerce du tableau à Paris : dans la seconde moitié du XVIIIe siècle ; acteurs et pratiques*. Villeneuve-D'ascq: Presses Univ. Du Septentrion.

Mylearning.org (2021) *The History of Papier Mâché*. Available at: <https://mylearning.org/stories/the-art-and-craft-of-papier-mch-/1009>. [Accessed 10 November 2021]

Popova, M. (2021) *The Surprising History of the Pencil*. Available at: <https://www.brainpickings.org/2013/06/24/history-of-the-pencil/> [Accessed 10 November 2021].

de Saint-Simon, H. (2018) *Opinions Litteraires, Philosophiques Et Industrielles (1825)*. Wentworth Press.

Sérullaz, M. and Graham, E. (1984) *The concise encyclopaedia of Impressionism*. Omega Press.

The Art Story (2021) *Avant-Garde Art - Modern Art Terms and Concepts*. Available at: <https://www.theartstory.org/definition/avant-garde/> [Accessed 10 November 2021].

The Art Story (2021) *Nouveau Réalisme Movement Overview.* Available at: <https://www.theartstory.org/movement/nouveau-realisme/> [Accessed 10 November 2021].

Worvill, R. (2010) 'From Prose peinture to Dramatic tableau: Diderot, Fénelon and the emergence of the pictorial aesthetic in France', in Thomas, D.A., Lisa Forman Cody and American Society For Eighteenth-Century Studies (ed.) *Studies in eighteenth-century culture.* Volume 39. Baltimore: Johns Hopkins University Press.

This chapter uses material from the following Wikipedia articles, which are released under the <https://creativecommons.org/licenses/by-sa/3.0/> Creative Commons Attribution-Share-Alike License 3.0.

<https://en.wikipedia.org/wiki/Art_Nouveau>

<https://en.wikipedia.org/wiki/Trompe-l%27%C5%93il>

<https://en.wikipedia.org/wiki/Papier-mâché>

<https://en.wikipedia.org/wiki/Collage>

[Accessed 10 November 2021].

# 5 - Politics

*Jenny Frendo and Graham Moore*

## Introduction

We have seen how the English language evolved after 1066 and assimilated many words of French origin. During the late 17th and 18th centuries, the period referred to as The Enlightenment (*Le siècle des lumières*), exchanges of ideas between European philosophers and writers saw the English adopt vocabulary associated with the politics of the period in France.

The term Enlightenment encompasses philosophies developed by thinkers in Britain, France, Germany and Switzerland. Diderot's *Encyclopédie* (1751–55) brought together writings by authors covering a wide range of issues including science, moral issues, natural history and religion. This wide-ranging work was notable for its attitudes of tolerance and liberalism.

# 5 - Politics

The philosophies of men such as David Hume, John Locke, Jean-Jacques Rousseau and Voltaire (to name just a few) were an important catalyst for the French Revolution. The Enlightenment followed by the upheaval and terrors in late 18th-century France have left a lasting impression on the English language.

### *Alien*

This is from Old French and means strange or foreign. It was used in this way in mid 15th-century England and was used to describe someone who was a foreigner living in England. In the 17th century it was also used to refer to something 'wholly different in nature' and it was not until the 1920s that the term 'alien' meant a being from another universe.

### *Ancien Régime*

This term was used when referring to the political/social system in France before the revolution of 1789. It is used today not solely in the socio-political sense but more generally to refer to institutions or systems that are seen as outdated. It is a description that implies disapproval.

### *Bourgeoisie*

This term dates from the early 18th century and was used in France to refer to freemen living in towns. It became used more generally to describe those who were middle class, generally town dwellers as opposed to peasants in the countryside. It was used in Marxist contexts in the late 19th century to describe the capitalist class i.e. those who owned wealth and the means of production which was associated with exploitation of the working classes. Today it is still used to describe the middle classes but it can sometimes be a disparaging term describing those who are perceived as materialistic and conventional.

### *Chauvinism*

This refers to excessive nationalistic fervour. Chauvin is said to have served in Napoleon's Grande Armée, was wounded 17 times and badly maimed. Napoléon presented him with the Sabre d'Honneur and a pension. He is reputed to have said 'The Old Guard dies but does not surrender'. At Waterloo it did and he (or the commander Pierre Cambronne) is thought to have actually merely said '*merde*'.

Chauvinism is now used for any excessive form of bigotry or bias. It is probable that Chauvin was not a real person, but a hero invented as an example to encourage men to give their all for the Glory of France

Chauvinism is now used for any excessive form of bigotry or bias, particularly sexual bias as in 'male chauvinist pig'.

### *Coup d'état*

Used in mid 17th-century France to describe a sudden, decisive political act referring to unexpected changes in forms and methods of government. In the present day it generally means the overthrow of a government and the illegal seizure of power.

### *Droit du Seigneur*

This term was brought to life in Beaumarchais's play *The Marriage of Figaro* and refers to a supposed Medieval custom that gave the Lord (*Seigneur*) the right to bed the bride of a vassal on their wedding night. Although in this play Beaumarchais was using the idea of *droit du seigneur* as a way of criticising the aristocracy, *The Marriage of Figaro* was a roaring success and very much enjoyed by many of those he was taking aim at. It is now thought that this right to 'bed the bride' was an invention of those (such as Beaumarchais) in the 18th century who wanted to discredit the ruling classes with the intention of bringing about change to the social order.

## *Émigré*

This term was used to describe royalists and others who fled the French Revolution in the late 18th century to take refuge overseas. By the late 19th century it was used more generally and now is used to refer to political exiles.

### *Entente Cordiale*

This commonly used term dates from the reign of Edward VII when the UK and France tried to calm the traditional rivalry of neighbours who for centuries had competed for influence in Europe and trading opportunities overseas. It consisted of a series of agreements signed on 8 April 1904 between the UK and France to counteract the rising power of Germany and to agree on many areas of dispute overseas. At that time the UK was the most powerful manufacturing and trading nation in Europe while France was the cultural capital, with Impressionist art, fashion and music pre-eminent. Paris was a great tourist destination for the King, aristocracy and bourgeoisie of Britain.

To the French the *Entente* tends today to be replaced with '*La perfide Albion*' (the French government protested that the

Eurostar link between Paris and London via the Eurotunnel terminated at Waterloo station!). Brexit and disputes over the export of COVID vaccines seem to confirm that to the French '*La perfide Albion*' is more appropriate than the now forgotten *Entente Cordiale*.

## *Jacobin*

The term Jacobin was originally used to refer to a Dominican Friar in 14th-century Paris who built the church of St Jacques. In the early stages of the French Revolution some of those who supported regime change met near the church and became known as Jacobins. This group had members with a number of differing ideas about the course that the revolution should take. As the revolution progressed and Robespierre came to prominence, radical members of the Jacobin club were drawn to his leadership and his desire to strengthen and deepen the radical ideals of the revolution. They represented the most extreme element in the revolutionary movement and in Britain the term Jacobin came to signify the worst excesses of revolution. Since then it has been used to describe those alleged to be involved in radical politics. The term Jacobin is used in a different way in France and refers to a system that sees a centralised administration run by bureaucrats and technocrats who hold sway over all geographical areas and social affairs in order to impose uniformity.

## *Laissez faire*

It is believed that from the late 17th century the term *laissez faire* (*laissez nous faire*) was used by French economists to refer to non-interference in commerce and the business of merchants. In 19th-century Britain the policy of *laissez faire* was embraced by politicians who believed that the economic system worked best when free from economic intervention such as regulations and subsidies. The system was attacked by Maynard Keynes in 1926 and debate over *laissez faire* policies continue to this day.

### *Provocateur*

The French term *agent provocateur* is used to describe someone hired to make trouble. This was shortened to *provocateur* and is used in Britain to refer to someone who commits damning and illegal acts in the name of a group in order to damage the reputation of that group.

# 6 – Music

*Michael Cutler and Peter Small*

## Introduction

The development of modern musical vocabularies stems from the new spirit awakened in Europe around 1500, giving a desire to learn more about the world we inhabit, and to revive and develop the artistic and cultural traditions that had effectively lain dormant for centuries. This movement initially flourished in the cities of Italy and, although it was initially called the *Risorgimento*, its route into English, as so often, came through the French word *Renaissance*.

In a musical context, the harsh disciplines of Catholic plain-song, which had been the standard music since the 6th century, began to relax, and a new harmony (Fr. *harmonie*) appeared. The new music quickly became popular, partly through its link to the French Troubadours, and had the effect of significantly reducing the Church's domination of music. As a result, music finally attained a respected position in European artistic life.

This wide acceptance was greatly boosted by the concurrent appearance of printed music. Music that had previously been available to only a small circle, could now be heard simultaneously throughout Europe. It is probably fair to say that this was music's most important leap forward until the arrival of the radio 400 years later.

## Language of music

The musical terminology that spread across Europe from the 16th century was predominantly Italian. This was because the principal new musical forms (opera and instrumental music) developed mainly in Italy. Furthermore, European countries hastened to import a substantial number of Italians to spread this new music in their own territories.

France, however, wishing to maintain its individual identity, developed its own musical forms:

- The baroque *suite*, a set of several contrasting instrumental pieces, usually based on dance forms. The dances were known by their French names, such as *sarabande, gavotte, minuet, gigue*.

- Ballet. The earliest *ballet de cour* was produced at the French court in 1581. Crucially, the form was adopted by Louis XIV, a known dance enthusiast. He established the Académie Royale de Danse, which set the standards and terminology for ballet companies throughout the world. (Oddly, the oldest ballets performed today date only from the mid 19th century and the emergence of the dominant figure of the ballerina (Italian!)). But the technical terms remained French, such as *arabesque, corps de ballet, pas de deux* and many others.

These French expressions have continued to be associated with these forms and have entered artistic vocabularies all over the world.

### *Arabesque*

A florid or ornamental piece of instrumental music in the Arabic style, for example the two *Arabesques* for piano by Debussy. The term is also used in ballet for a position in which (incredibly) one leg is raised behind and the arms are extended.

### *Cor Anglais*

A woodwind instrument related to the oboe. Despite the name it is not a horn and it didn't originate in England! This instrument originated in 16th century Germany where it was given the name *Engellisches Horn* meaning 'Angelic Horn'. It is thought that because *Engellisch* also meant 'English', over time 'Angelic Horn' became 'English Horn' and hence *Cor Anglais*.

### *Corps de ballet*

This is the basic troupe of a ballet company supporting the 58 principal dancers, particularly in classical ballet, for example the swans in Swan Lake. The corps de ballet reflects the style and importance of the company and is the result of years of hard training. A ballet star can be recruited, but there is no such thing as an 'instant' corps de ballet.

### *Étude*

This means a 'study' in French. In music, it was initially designed as a short piece merely to develop technique in playing a solo instrument, particularly the piano. However, some composers, notably Chopin, composed *études* of such quality and virtuosity that they have entered into concert programmes.

### *Pas de deux*

All steps in ballet are known by the French word *pas*. *Pas de deux* is one of several in which the actual number of dancers is indicated (two in this case). It is often a highlight of a performance involving the two leading dancers. The name of a step can also often indicate its character as in *pas de chat*, which emulates the pouncing jump of a cat.

### *Nocturne*

In French this word means 'pertaining to night'. In music, a short piece for piano, suggesting a nocturnal, often dreamy, atmosphere. The style and name were first used by the Irish pianist and composer John Field, before Chopin adopted the term and produced 19 widely known examples.

### *Pirouette*

This is the French for a spinning top. This step involves one or more complete revolutions of the body, performed on one leg, with the point of the working leg usually touching the knee of the supporting leg. Warning: Don't try this at home!

# 7 – Sport and Games

*Michael Cutler and Peter Small*

## Introduction

In France sports such as football and rugby are hugely popular and the French have been highly successful on the international sporting stage. So perhaps it is a bit surprising that so few sporting words and expressions used in English are actually French. In Victorian England there was a drive to write down and standardise the rules and regulations of sports, especially those played in the public schools. These sports and their rules were then readily exported around the British Empire along with the creation of clubs and competitions.

So by the early 20th century football, rugby, cricket and many other sports were being played around the world between teams using agreed rules, leading to the great success of these sports. When we consider football, the most popular sport in the world, historians have found evidence of early versions from China through to Ancient Greece. But it is the version standardised in England that dominates the world today. Like rugby, the football game played around the world was originally played in English public schools in the 19th century, where the rules and regulations were written down and agreed so that schools could compete against each other. This led to the establishment of sports clubs and competitions that soon spread around the world thanks to the British Empire. Sports clubs were being established in France as well, e.g. Racing Club de France, sometimes following the English model. These sports clubs often played football, rugby and athletics whose rules and terminology had already been established in England.

We need to look at sports and games which have been heavily influenced by the French in order to find words that have been adopted into English.

Tennis is a sport which is thought to be descended from a game played without rackets in 12th-century France called *jeu de paume*. Over many years this was exported to England where it became known as 'real tennis' or 'royal tennis'. This game was hugely popular with royalty in 16th-century France and England. Real tennis is still played today in Europe and the USA and much of the terminology used in real tennis is French (*le dedans, le trou, la lune*). So here we have an international sport whose French origins are clear and the original French words are still used.

# 7 – Sport and Games

But in 1874 a different version of tennis called 'lawn tennis' was invented by an Englishman, Walter Wingfield. This game was much more accessible by ordinary people because it could be played on grass rather than requiring a specially-built court. Lawn Tennis was adopted by the All England Club and very soon it had spread worldwide leaving Real Tennis as very much a minority sport. In France of course, French words are used in lawn tennis (e.g. *une faute, égalité, avantage*) but the rules are the same as those previously established in the UK, so unsurprisingly no French words moved back into English.

Even with a sport like cycling (is there a more famous cycling event than the Tour de France?) the terminology most used in the sport in the UK remains relentlessly English.

Early bicycles were simple devices propelled by the rider pushing his feet against the ground. The first properly rideable bicycle was invented by a Scot, Kirkpatrick Macmillan in 1839, using foot cranks. Almost immediately, these new machines were being used for bicycle races especially in Britain and France. In France, the touring style of racing developed whereas in Britain, probably because of the more restrictive road regulations, time trials and track racing were more the norm. In 1900 the Union Cycliste Internationale was established in France to control the rules and regulations of all types of competitive cycling but by this time bicycles and cycle racing had already been well established in the UK so largely retained the existing English words. The Tour de France remains perhaps the most important cycling competition in the world, however, and English audiences are accustomed to seeing *pelotons* of riders on television.

# 7 – Sport and Games

One of the most ancient and widely-played board games in the world is chess. Chess spread with remarkably few changes from 7th-century India where it is thought to have been invented, to Persia and North Africa, and thence via the Arab world into Europe hundreds of years later. At that point the terminology used in the game was predominantly European-ised versions of the Arabic or Persian words. For instance the French name for chess, *échecs*, thought to be derived from the Persian word shah meaning 'king'. When *échecs* arrived in England from France, the word *échecs* was transformed into 'chess'.

In the 15th century the rules in Europe were modified and standardised, probably in France. At this point it acquired some new terminology in the French and German languages, such as a new *en passant* rule. These new rules eventually became adopted in the standard game of chess now played all over the world with a governing body called the Fédération Internationale des Échecs, based in Switzerland. [4]

Skiing has become one of the most popular types of holiday for British people who love the idea of sun-kissed glamorous alpine ski resorts. Skiing as a sport first took off in Norway in the 19th century. It was developed further by the French, especially after the first Winter Olympics in Chamonix in 1924. This helped to create the idea of a glamorous skiing lifestyle and tiny villages like Chamonix and Val d'Isère were transformed into ski resorts over the subsequent years. Of course, the holiday-makers soon picked up the language of the ski slope and brought words like piste, avalanche and *après-ski* back to Britain with them where they rapidly became part of everyday English.

# 7 – Sport and Games

Some would say that Ian Fleming's James Bond character, as popularised in postwar novels and films, played a large part in this glamorisation of skiing with so many scenes involving skis and snow. But James Bond also had a penchant for gambling and casinos, as depicted in the novel Casino Royale. Perhaps this helped to glamorise casinos as well! The game most associated with casinos is probably roulette. Roulette developed in France, getting its name from the French expression 'little wheel'. It is claimed that the famous scientist and mathematician Blaise Pascal may have been involved in developing roulette. The story goes that his quest for a perpetual motion machine led to the game's nearly frictionless spinning wheel. Although there are many versions of roulette to be found in casinos around the world, they are all descended from the French roulette played in France and Monte Carlo, presided over by a *croupier*. However, in English-speaking countries much of the French terminology of roulette has been replaced by equivalent English terms.

### *Après-Ski*

Usually used in French to refer to a snow boot. Following the growth in popularity in skiing holidays after World War 2, the term came to be used to refer to the various social activities that take place after a day's skiing – usually involving alcohol. The term has become widely used and understood around the world, including in English.

### *Croupier*

Nowadays this refers to someone who works at a casino, whose job is to assist at the gambling tables and to collect and pay debts. From the Old French word croupier meaning someone who backs up a gambler with extra cash if needed. This was derived from the French word *croupe* meaning the rump (of a horse), so you can imagine that a croupier was 'standing on the back' of the gambler.

### *Dressage*

Equine sport involving tests of horsemanship. Dressage means 'training' in French.

### *En garde*

A term used in the sport of fencing; it is a warning call to competitors to prepare for action. Meaning 'on guard', it is borrowed from French and has found its way into general English usage.

### *En passant*

Meaning 'in passing' in French, this term was borrowed by the game of chess (probably in the 15th century) to refer to a move where a pawn that makes its first two-square move can be captured by an opponent's pawn as if it had only moved one square. So, the opposing pawn is captured while 'passing through' the usual square from where it would ordinarily be liable to be captured.

### *Grand Prix*

A race or competition typically at the highest level. From the French meaning 'Great Prize'. It is thought that it was first used in the famous horse-racing championship at Longchamps, the 'Grand Prix de Paris'. The name Grand Prix is now used for many international races and events, especially in Formula 1 racing.

### *Hors de combat*

Translates from French as 'out of the fight' or 'out of action', this term refers to military personnel who are no longer able to be combatants. In general English usage, the term has come to refer to any situation where someone is no longer able to carry out an activity, or continue playing in a sporting activity.

### *Peloton*

The main group of riders in a cycle race, grouped close together to save energy. In French, the word also means 'platoon', a small group of soldiers.

### *Piste*

In French piste means a path or trail, including a downhill ski run. The ski run is the meaning that has been adopted into English.

## Conclusion

So in conclusion it is evident that there are three things which influence the 'language' of a sport or game – the place where it originated, the place where the rules are written down and standardised, and the way in which the sport or game spread around the world. Skiing, cycling, chess and roulette: all have been heavily influenced early on by the French and it seems that is why some of these words have made it into everyday English.

## References

'Chess' in *Encyclopaedia Britannica* (1970), vol. 5.

Le Point (2015) *Le jeu de paume, le sport des rois qui traverse le temps*. Available at: <https://www.lepoint.fr/sport/le-jeu-de-paume-le-sport-des-rois-qui-traverse-le-temps-17-04-2015-1922314_26.php> [Accessed 10 November 2021].

'Roulette' in *Encyclopaedia Britannica* (1970), vol. 19.

'Tennis' in *Encyclopaedia Britannica* (1970), vol. 21.

Time (2019) *Now You Know: Why Is Tennis Scored So Weirdly?* Available at: <https://time.com/5040182/tennis-scoring-system-history/> [Accessed 10 November 2021].

# 8 - Travel and Tourism

*Gay Umney and Gill Saunders*

After consulting several holiday *brochures* I made a *reservation* at a charming lakeside hotel on the Baltic Sea. Armed with my *passport*, *visa* and *ticket*, I took off from the airport and on arrival in Sofia loaded my *baggage* into a hired *automobile*. En route to my destination I took a *detour* to admire a famous *château* and visited a friend who has a *pied-à-terre* in the nearby *village*. My *voyage* took me through an historic tunnel and on a *circuit* of ancient city walls. At the hotel the *concierge* arranged for my luggage to be taken to my *suite*, which had an idyllic view over the lake. During my stay I enjoyed the fine *cuisine* and *gourmet* dining in the many restaurants around the lake and was able to buy *souvenirs* from the *kiosk* in the *pavilion* on the *promenade*.

# 8 - Travel and Tourism

The words and expressions highlighted in the paragraph above are frequently used in everyday English yet are of French origin. This is just a small example of how our languages intertwine and we are often unaware that we are speaking French.

The majority of native English speakers today would not recognize the following words associated with travel as 'foreign' because they have become a part of our everyday lexicon. As such they have been adopted as our own, but their roots can be traced back through the centuries to borrowings from the French language, with a significant enrichment to the English vocabulary.

The English word 'foreign' has its roots firmly in 13th-century France, from Old French *forain* meaning 'strange or of persons outside the boundaries of a country'. It is no longer in use in current French, having been replaced by *étrangère*.

Nowadays, a *forain* in French is an owner or employee of large and small attractions, rides, fairground stands, and market stalls. As fairground businesses are mostly family owned, the term *forain* is applied by extension to the family of these people. The communities they form are generally associated with travellers. They have no fixed abode and are therefore in a way 'strangers' in the places where they stay briefly.

## 'Voyage' versus 'Travel'

The English verb 'to travel', meaning 'to go from one place to another', is used in everyday English to describe a mode of transport or a journey taken. In fact, 'travel' actually takes its source from the 13th-century French *travailen*, meaning 'to work strenuously, trouble or to journey'. The most numerous travellers in history to bring French words into the English spoken language were the traders. Amongst them, artisans, merchants, carpenters and tailors all contribute to today's English vocabulary. From 1670–1710 the French speaking Calvinist Huguenot population was forced to flee France and many arrived in the UK, bringing their trades and language to the UK. The French word *réfugié*, the modern day equivalent to the English word 'refugee', was first used to describe their arrival.

Back in the 16th century, during the Anglo-French wars, England borrowed much from French military language. Such loan words still exist. For example, 'army', 'enemy', 'battle', 'siege', 'defence', 'manoeuvre', 'bivouac', 'corps', 'terrain', 'soldier', 'guard' and the ranks of officers. It would be virtually impossible to describe current military affairs without this linguistic influence. In fact, the English word 'war' is one of the earliest words derived from the French *guerre*, the initial 'w' being due to dialectal origin.

In the 17th and 18th centuries, educational tours on the continent were fashionable for young men of good social standing. Paris was the most popular sojourn of the Grand Tour for its cultural, architectural, and linguistic influence as indeed many British elite had already studied classical French literature. In fact the word 'tourist' was first used in 1772 and is in part a derivative of old French *torner*, a 'turn', 'circuit', or 'round'. Evolving from this stem, the word 'tourism' was first noted in 1811.

# 8 - Travel and Tourism

So we can see that foreign travel has had an undisputed influence on the English language and there are many words now so naturalised in English that they can be used without a second thought. In the words of Jules Verne: 'Travel enables us to enrich our lives with new experiences, to enjoy and to be educated, to learn respect for foreign cultures, to establish friendships, and above all to contribute to international cooperation and peace throughout the world.' Bon voyage!

### *Adventure*

Breaking this down to the basic form, we can see its origin in Latin and Old French, *ad+venir*: *ad* 'to' + *venir* 'come'. The French written form reduced simply to *à venture*, 'that which happens by chance, fortune or luck'.

### *Baggage*

'Baggage' first appeared in the English lexicon in the 15th century from the Old French *bagage* meaning 'property picked up for transport'. Its roots lie in the Old French verb *baguer*, 'to tie up'. These appear to come from the same source as our English 'bag', but this is suspected to be of Norse origin. Rather, the origin lies in the French *bague* meaning a 'bundle or sack' with the added '-age' suffix to indicate action.

### *Brochure*

Dating to the mid-18th century in France when small books or pamphlets were produced by stitching pages together. The word 'brochure' comes from the French *brocher* meaning to stitch. Roots can be further traced back to the Old French *brochier*, 'to pierce', and *broche*, 'awl', revealing the true origin of the handcrafted brochure. Holiday brochures, usually folded and containing summary information, first emerged in the UK in the 1830s with the burgeoning market for overseas tourism. However, today's demand for paper holiday brochures has declined with the demand for on-line travel bookings.

### Ticket

An early 16th-century English word shortened from the French *etiquet* meaning a little note stuck or affixed to a gate or a wall as a public notice; or, in the 21st century, stuck to the window of a car as a parking ticket or *PV* (*procès verbal*) in French! The meaning of 'ticket' as a card or piece of paper giving a right or privilege was first recorded in the 17th century. The English pronunciation drops the 'e' from *étiquette* so the word is pronounced 'tiquette'.

*Avoir un ticket* ('to be fancied') is a French idiomatic expression that means to be attracted to someone. This expression has been used quite commonly since the middle of the 20th century. It means that someone likes you, especially physically. Indeed, in slang, the 'ticket' is a mark of physical interest, even purely sexual.

### Billet

Word dating from the 15th century. It comes from the middle English *bylet* and from the Anglo-French *billette*, diminutive of *bille* ('bill') or ('log') of Celtic origin: akin to Old Irish *bile* meaning 'landmark tree'.

The word *billet* (pronounced 'billette') used in French in the English sense of 'ticket' is a false friend. It has been used in English since the 15th century in its original meaning of military accommodation or billeting. The word 'ticket' has long since ceased to be used in French to designate the title of travel by train (*un billet de train*) or plane (*un billet d'avion*). The only one that has survived is the metro ticket (*un ticket de métro*). We also speak of a cinema ticket and a theatre ticket (*un billet de théâtre et un billet de cinéma*). Some idiomatic expressions such as a love letter (*un billet doux*) adds a touch of ambiguity for English-speaking learners.

### *Circuit*

The noun 'circuit' meaning a boundary line going around an area, whether circular or not, comes from the Old French *circuit* and stems from the Latin *circuitis*. The verb meaning 'to journey around a particular place or area' dates from the early 15th century.

### *Detour*

18th-century verb from the old French *destorner*, turn aside. The noun means a side road or byway, which is often where foreign motorists get hopelessly lost when following a *déviation* sign in France!

### *Historic*

First found in mid-17th century English and possibly influenced by the French word *historique*. Beware! Don't forget that in French the letter 'h' is silent.

# 8 - Travel and Tourism

## *Hotel*

Originating in Old French *ostel* meaning a lodging. By the mid-17th century *un hotel* was a mansion, large house or private residence.

One of the most common and easily understood words for travellers, regardless of language, is 'hotel'. Derived from the French *hôtel* with the same origin as 'hospital', the original meaning was of a building providing care for frequent visitors, rather than its contemporary use as a place of accommodation. The French circumflex replaces the 's' found in the earlier hostel spelling, with the English dropping the use of the circumflex altogether.

These words are related to French *hote* (*hôte*) or 'host' and the word stem refers to Latin *hospes*, 'guest'. In 17th-century France, the town houses of the nobility were known as French hotels for the *hôtel particulier*.

Be careful of the *Hôtel de ville* or the *Hôtel de police*. They are indeed public places but do not try to book a room in these places.

## *Pied à terre*

The literal translation, 'foot on the ground', first appeared in France in the early 18th century. Referring to a small town house or rooms used for short residences, it was adopted by the English a century later. These days the ownership of secondary residences, which are often left empty for long periods of time, is controversial in large cities where there is a shortage of housing stock.

# 8 - Travel and Tourism

### *Tunnel*

In the early 15th century a *tonel* was a funnel-shaped net for catching birds, from *tonelle* the old French word for a 'net'. The sense of 'tunnel' as an underground passage first appeared in the mid-17th century in England and was subsequently adopted into French. A *tonnelle* is a 'gazebo' in French.

### *Kiosk*

The French *kiosque* is a 17th-century word meaning an open pavilion made of wood and often supported by pillars. It originated in Persia and appeared in both languages in the 17th century. Kiosks were introduced into Europe as ornaments in gardens and parks. In the mid-19th century. the word came to be used for street news-stands and in the early 20th century telephone 'kiosks' were introduced.

### *Passport*

Originating in 15th-century France, *passe-port* derives from the French *passer*, 'to pass', and *port*, 'port', and gave authorisation to travel, enter or leave a country.

Centuries ago, the *sauf conduit* or 'safe conduct pass' was designed to grant an enemy passage in and out of a kingdom for the purpose of his negotiations. This was little more than a written plea that acted as a type of gentleman's agreement that no war would ensue.

### *Pavilion*

An early 13th-century word for a large tent raised on posts and used as a movable habitation. It came from the Old French *paveillon* or *papillon* ('butterfly') because of its resemblance to butterfly wings. From the 17th century the word was also used to describe an open building in a public space for shelter and entertainment.

The modern French meaning has moved away from the Old French and modern English meaning in the 20th century. It describes a private isolated building, situated in a property, a park like a hunting lodge (*pavillon de chasse*) or a ward in a hospital (*le pavillon Berlioz*) Nowadays, it also describes a private house, of small or medium size, attached to a plot of land and located in particular on the outskirts of large cities.

### *Promenade*

A mid-16th century English word for 'a place for walking', taken from the French *se promener* meaning a leisurely walk taken for pleasure or display. From the 17th century it referred particularly to a walkway by the sea. A famous promenade is *La Promenade des Anglais* in Nice.

### *Souvenir*

This 12th-century French word describes a remembrance or memory from the Old French noun *souvenir*. With roots in Old French and Latin, it can be seen to be a combination of *sub* and *venire*, 'up from below' and 'to come'. As far back as the late 17th century 'the Grand Tour' was a trip taken by upper class young men and women, with the goal of exposing them to the artistic riches of France and Italy. These long sojourns (*séjours*) became a custom of the socially elite of Europe and as part of this tradition travellers would collect artwork and souvenirs as mementos of their travels.

The modern meaning of the French word *souvenir* generally describes small objects of little value sold to tourists. It is also used to indicate an object that recalls the memory of someone or an event.

### *Voyage*

The English word 'voyage' is used to describe a trip or journey and stems from the 12th-century French word *voiage* meaning an 'errand, mission or crusade'. When we look more closely at the root of the word, it is interesting to see links to the French *vie* ('life') and the Latin *via* ('way'), and adding the suffix 'age' creates an action, perfectly bringing together the action of taking a personal journey. It was originally adopted into Middle English as *viage*.

Of course, we all wish for a 'good journey' so the phrase *bon voyage* had been readily integrated into English from its first-known use around 1670.

As in English, the term *voyage* ('journey') has the meaning of going to or being transported to another place; a journey thus made. For example, a journey by boat (*voyager par bateau*), or to feel the fatigues of travel (*ressentir les fatigues du voyage*).

However, in modern French, it describes rather the action of going to a relatively distant or foreign place. One often speaks of a 'sojourn' (*séjour*) or *un voyage* ('a journey/a trip'). The expression *aimer les voyages* evokes a liking of distant and exotic destinations.

## References

Harper, D., 2021. Etymonline - Online Etymology Dictionary. [online] Available at: <https://www.etymonline.com/> [Accessed 11 November 2021].

Merriam-webster.com (2019), Merriam-Webster Dictionary. [online] Available at: https://www.merriam-webster.com/dictionary [Accessed 10 November 2021].

# 8 - Travel and Tourism

# 9 – Fashion

*David Turnbull*

Why do people wear clothes? Stop sniggering at the back!

Let's start again. Why do Europeans, and particularly the two countries either side of the Channel, dress like they do and to what extent do styles of dress and the words used to describe them cross geographical boundaries?

As humans moved north out of Africa it became necessary to cover themselves to keep warm for most of the time. Since then, as well as for protection, clothing has become used for modesty, identification, decoration and to display status. When looking at all these reasons, apart from the last two, most languages have their own unique words for the bits and bobs involved. For the English speaking the words hat, sock, skirt, shirt and coat exist in the singular and can be made plural by adding an 's' but trousers, tights and knickers exist only in the plural.

However, as soon as decoration and status become involved, French and its associated grammar seems to dominate the vocabulary and we will cover this point eventually a couple of paragraphs further on.

For most of the 18th, 19th and early 20th centuries changes in day-to-day clothing styles rarely crossed from one country to another. A good example of this is the overall *bleu de travail* and *salopette* of the French worker in factories and on the land. The British relied much more on hand-me-downs from their social betters. One of the few examples of internationalism concerned, reportedly, the bootmakers of Northampton who kept the Napoleonic armies shod. Indeed, they protested loudly when the British government banned the trade. These protests were nowhere near as loud as those coming from the French infantry sent to Russia in boots with cardboard soles.

In the decades following the end of the last world war Anglo Saxons had a disproportionate influence on international popular culture like music, cinema and styles of dress. This has had a huge spin-off effect on how people behave and what they wear but beyond 'jeans' and 'pull' (a diminutive of pullover) very few clothing-related words were exported at this time whilst literally hundreds of words of French origin dominated the English fashion scene.

Some of these French words were pretty factual, cotton fabric from Nîmes was rightly called 'Denim'. *Broderie Anglaise* is, obviously, a French word to describe a popular type of English decorative stitching that was generally limited to Victorian underwear until Brigitte Bardot adopted it for a wedding dress.

The opulence of the grand French fashion houses and their Haute Couture was, of course, well known in England but was not followed as enthusiastically as some might have hoped, probably in no small part due to the Royal Family sticking with British designers. As dressing for pleasure grew and London became a world centre for the young it became necessary to attach more and more exotic names to the goods on sale. Lingerie sounds much more chic than foundation garments. Stylish gave way to *à la Mode*. Chain shops' ready-to-wear ranges became instantly more attractive as *Prêt à Porter*. Green and red couldn't do justice as exciting colours so had to reappear as *vert* and *rouge* along with *noir, cerise, beige* and *blanche*. When £1 for a T-shirt was seen as expensive it was more attractive to refer to any attached design as *appliqué* rather than as 'stuck on' or as 'a transfer'.

Many people of these two countries would be hard pressed to think of many English fashion words in use in France. Fear not, L'Académie Française has found some and announced alternatives; street wear ('trainers' to the over-forties) should become *la mode de la rue*. A pop-up store by definition a transient operation has now become established as *une boutique éphémère*. Top models, surely an easily understood descriptive phrase, are to be *mannequins vedettes*.

France and the French are still seen as the epitome of elegance but, subject to the paragraph above, the interchange of words associated with fashion appears to be more linked to the status and decorative aspects of clothing rather than as supportive of anything more fundamental.

# 10 - Literature and Drama

*Daphne Davidson-Kelly and Jenny Frendo*

Literature is the mirror into the soul, the personality, character and language of the nation wherein it is produced. Within the tapestry of literature we can see words which stayed from foreign influence or invasion, and those which strayed into the language at a later date, giving rise to a cry of: 'there's an *étranger* in my language' (Emily Eells 2013).

English is a hybrid language with many linguistic imports from invasions or simply adopted or appropriated because another language seems to better express a thought. Why foreign words are chosen over the vernacular would be an interesting study.

It is thought that there are about 7,000 French words in the English language today. However there are a further 10,000

# 10 - Literature and Drama

English words that have their roots in French and Latin and two thirds of the English is of French origin.

French influence on English literature seems to have come in waves. We can map out, rightly or wrongly, three waves: the Norman Conquest, the 17th and 18th centuries (French *Siècle des Lumières* and onwards) and finally the twentieth century.

Many words of French origin introduced during the Norman conquest form the bedrock of English and we hardly notice that they may be of French origin now so firmly are they are so well integrated.

The first wave of French words came with the conquest of England by William of Normandy, when Norman French become the language of Court politics and the law.

Norman French words were assimilated largely by the oral tradition as (manuscript) written material was the province of the clergy, jurists and administrators such as those who wrote up the Domesday book.

However its influence waned and by the time of Chaucer (1340–1400), 'the father of English literature', the English vernacular was established and French, apart from law, the church and politics, was scarcely used.

# 10 - Literature and Drama

Despite English Kings from William I to Henry VI marrying into French royalty or nobility[1] (except for William II (William Rufus) who did not marry) with a gap until Charles I, who married Henriette Marie of France, these consorts seem to have little effect on the language, literature or poetry of the time. Their influence was for the most part on politics and etiquette. The main exception to this might be Eleanor of Aquitaine (Queen of Henry II) who resurrected the ancient myths and legends of Arthur and Guinevere and the ideals and ideas of courtly love that were illustrated or illuminated in manuscripts. French words used in the legends largely related to heraldry, armour and arms, such as *cuir bouille* (hardened leather) *escutcheon, bordure, Joyeux* (Lancelot's sword), *jupon, honi soit qui mal y pense* ('shame on him who thinks evil' recorded from 1300 and used as the motto for the Order of the Garter).

According to Wikipedia, in 1328, when Charles IV of France died without an heir, Edward III of England and Philip VI of France disputed the French throne. This led to the Hundred Years' War, which provoked negative feelings towards French in England, whereupon French came to be seen as the language of the enemy. English reasserted itself as the language of govern-

---

1    Henry I: Matilda of Scotland then Adeliza of Louvain
     Henry II: Eleanor of Aquitaine
     Richard I: Berengaria of Navarre
     John: Isabella of Angouleme
     Henry III: Eleanor of Provence
     Edward I: Eleanor of Castile then Margaret of France
     Edward II: Isabella of France
     Edward III: Philippa of Hainault
     Richard II: Isabella of Valois
     Henry IV: Joan of Navarre

ment and learning after over 200 years as a language of low prestige.

In 1349, English became the language of instruction at the University of Oxford, which had previously taught in French or Latin.

The use of English became widespread by the introduction of printing in England by William Caxton in 1476. Henry IV (1367–1413) was the first English king whose first language was English, and Henry V (1387–1422) was the first king of England to use English in official documents. By being printed, words became 'legitimised' in the sense that they were taken as the recognised lexicon or language of England.

The first novels (an Italian word *novella*) were not printed until the middle 1700s: *Robinson Crusoe* (1719) by Daniel Defoe, *Joseph Andrews* (1742) and *Tom Jones* (1749) by Henry Fielding, and the scurrilous *Fanny Hill* (1748) by John Cleland. These set the way for the use of elaborate and decorative language freed from political and religious tracts (*belles lettres*).

The second wave of French words, facilitated by being printed, arrived in the 18th century when French ideas and books came to England influencing its art, poetry and literature from the dazzling Court of Louis XIV, and the French Enlightenment (Corneille, Racine, Molière and Voltaire – the *Philosophes*). The French Revolution brought ideals of the rights of man, liberty equality and fraternity, as well as ideas of social class (Bourgeoisie – the middle class of society). These ideas and principles influenced ideology, style, content and form of literature in England rather than lexicon.

# 10 - Literature and Drama

The educated and wealthier public travelled more and more, and authors and writers began to use and import foreign words, in particular French, to better express an emotion or an idea, or to add a certain *cachet* and a greater meaning to language. We can see words that were originally introduced or borrowed to enrich, stayed and fell into the ordinary idiolect of the language. Taking the novel by Thomas Hardy, *The Mayor of Caster-bridge* (1886) as a random snapshot in time, we can see French words and phrases used because they had become accepted as part of the idiolect, or they may have been used to impress or add dramatic effect. For example the eponymous Mayor is described as a man whose face is red with black eyes and then when angered he is described as turning '*rouge et noir*.' The use of French may have been to avoid repetition, or to add a sense of otherness, or to add drama. The onomatopoeic effect of the words '*rouge et noir*' is so much more sinister and volcanic than the bland 'red and black'. The music of the prose can be enhanced or enriched by *un mot étranger*. In the same work are to be found words such as c*arrefour* (crossroad), c*hassez-déchassez chassé* (dance step), *éclat* (burst), *espaliers* (method of training usually fruit trees), and *fête carillonne*. French words were used originally perhaps to enrich and thereafter became mundane and in commonplace use.

A third wave of French words and phrases arrived in the 20th century after two world wars and the financial crisis and the aftermath. Literature became more and more internationalised. French words used in diplomacy (*entente cordial, cordon sanitaire, denouement, parvenu, hors de combat, impasse*) and trade, commerce and political theory (*laissez-faire*, as popularised by Adam Smith) became part of the language of literature. The works of Sartre, Camus, Gide and Simenon were translated and had a huge impact on thought and philosophy and lexicon. French words and phrases that better defined ideas or philosophies were commonly used, such as:

- *Déjà vu* (already seen – the phenomenon of feeling something has been seen or done before when at the same time one is sure one has not done either)
- *Amour propre* (self respect)
- *Au contraire* (on the contrary)
- *Avant-garde* (ahead of its time)
- *Enfant terrible* (outrageous, troublesome or embarrassing person)
- *Coup de foudre* (love at first sight)
- *Gaffe* (mistake blunder)
- *Risqué* (daring)
- *Mot juste* (just the right word for the right occasion)
- *Acte gratuit* (a gratuitous act done on impulse often with tragic consequences)
- *Bon mot* (clever remark)
- *En rapport* (harmonious)
- *Double entendre* (word play or pun, which has lost its original meaning)
- *Chacun à son goût* (each to his own taste)
- *Femme fatale* (come to mean a dangerously alluring attractive woman)
- *Crime passionnel* (crime of passion)
- *Idée fixe* (fixation or obsession)
- *Habitué* (resident or habitual visitor to a place)

- *Malaise* (discontent)
- *Roman à clef* (an account of an actual person disguised as a fictional persona)

French words and phrases somehow better expressed the new ideas ranging from existentialism, realism, and the psychological exploration of the criminal mind (e.g., Simenon) even the mood of the time. There was no reason to translate these words and phrases which were so appropriately appropriated *juste à point*.

The globalisation of the world with easy travel and communication has led to the integration of *mots et phrases étrangers* some of which having served their purpose have fallen by the wayside, or lost their original meaning having been so integrated as to have become expressive of a purely English sentiment (e.g., *double entendre*).

French words and phrases have enriched the English language in literature perhaps because France has had the longest shared history and has been part of the English culture – for better or for worse – for so long that it seems there is, and always will be, a respect for the French expression because of its philosophical expression, resonance, cadence or because of its succinct expression of an idea or an ideal. Very often the *mot juste* required seems to be *à la française*.

There follows a selection of French words and phrases which we would not be surprised to meet in a novel or a work of prose or a *critique* of such. These have been roughly separated into words originally imported or appropriated, and then later words coming in on the crest of the second and third waves.

## Earlier imports up to 17th Century forming the bedrock of the language and literature

### *Grief*

Old French *grief*, from *grever* 'to burden'.

The first records of the word 'grief' come from around 1200. It ultimately comes from the Latin verb *gravāre*, meaning 'to burden', from *gravis*, 'heavy'. The same root forms the basis of the words 'gravity' and the adjective 'grave' meaning 'serious'.

Grievance in English has the meaning of a complaint against an injury and a wrong especially in legal terms.

### *Conceal*

From early English 14/15th centuries *concelen,* meaning 'to keep close or secret, forbear to divulge', to 'hide' or 'shield from observation'. Also from Old French *conceler* to hide. Replaced old English *deagan*.

### *Foreign*

From Old French *forain* (from Vulgar Latin *forānus*, from Latin *forīs* ('outside')). The current English spelling 'foreign' arose in the 16th century.

In French, *foire* ('fair'), once meant 'foreign', but has been replaced by *étranger* in this sense (see the chapter on Travel and Tourism).

### *Bienséance*

The word *bienséance* is an old word which came into English from French in the 17th Century. Derives from an old French verb, *seoir*, meaning 'to be suitable for' or 'to be appropriately situated' – which is also the origin of *séance*, which literally means 'a sitting'. A *séance* or seance is an attempt to communicate with spirits. The word *séance* comes from the French word for 'session', from the Old French *seoir*, 'to sit'. In French, the word's meaning is quite general: one may, for example, speak of *une séance de cinema*.

The word *bienséance* means 'decorum', 'propriety', or 'social decency'.

### Buffet

According to the bilingual *Dictionarie of the French and English Tongues* (1611), *bouffage* means 'any meat that (eaten greedily) fills the mouth and makes the cheeks to swell'.

A *bouffage* is a satisfying meal or feast. 'Buffet' is a modern usage.

### Farouche

The adjective 'farouche' derives directly from French *farouche*. It probably derives from a Latin word meaning 'living outside'. Because of the timid behaviour of wild animals, however, in English *farouche* tends to be used to mean 'shy' or 'socially reserved' and by extension 'sullen' or 'ill-humoured'.

### Froideur

French word for 'coldness', but in English is used more figuratively to refer to a 'cooling' or 'chilling' of a relationship – and in particular a business or diplomatic one.

### *Badineur*

French *badiner*, 'to tease'. In use in English as 'badinage' to refer to witty, playful banter since the mid-1600s.

Much less well known is the word for someone who indulges in precisely that: namely, a 'badineur'. Also in the sophisticated 'badinage' of the characters in plays by Oscar Wilde.

### *Embonpoint*

Late 17th century. From French *en bon point*, 'in good condition'. In English usage, *embonpoint* refers to the plump or fleshy part of a person's body, in particular a woman's bosom or a man's paunch. For example, '*I have lost my embonpoint, and become quite thin*' (Jerdan 1838).

### *Bizarre*

First recorded in 1640–50, from the French *bizarre* meaning 'fantastical, odd, strange'. Originally from Italian *bizzarro*. The Italian meaning evolved to mean 'unpredictable, eccentric', then 'strange, weird', in which sense it was taken into French and then English. The word is used as an adjective meaning markedly unusual in appearance, style, or general character and often involving incongruous or unexpected elements; outrageously or whimsically strange.

## Since 17th Century

### *À Contrecoeur*

French: *contre* 'against', *coeur* 'heart'.

First used in English around the turn of the 19th century. To do something *à contrecoeur* is to do it reluctantly, or against your will or better judgement; it literally means 'against your heart'.

### *Aperçu*

A form of the French word *apercevoir*, 'to perceive'.

An *aperçu* is a telling insight or a quick, revealing glimpse of something. It appears early in the 19th Century in English.

### *Arrière-Pensée*

French, literally a 'back-thought'.

*Arrière-pensée* is another word for what we might otherwise call 'an ulterior motive'.

### *Arriviste*

*Arriviste* has been used in English since the early 1900s. It comes from the French word *arriver* 'to arrive'.

It essentially means 'arrival' or 'arriver', but is typically used specifically in the sense of someone intent on making a name for themselves, or else a brash, conspicuous newcomer yet to fit into their new surroundings.

*The Arriviste* is a work by Marjorie Ena Mary Taylor on the origins and evolution of the 'arriviste' in the 19th Century French Novel, with particular reference to Stendhal and Balzac (*Père Goriot*), Becky Sharp in Vanity Fair. William Makepeace Thackeray was an arriviste.

### *Attentisme*

Derived from French *attendre* meaning 'to wait' or 'an expectation' (*une attente*). *Attentisme* is another word for patience or perseverance, or else what we'd more likely refer to as 'the waiting game'.

### *Croquis*

Derived from a French verb meaning 'to sketch', a *croquis* is a quick drawing or a character sketch in a novel, a rough draft of something to be improved on later.

### *Débouché*

The French verb *déboucher* means 'to clear' or 'unblock', or by extension 'to uncork a bottle'. Derived from that, the English verb 'debouch' means to move from an enclosed space to an open one, and in that sense has been used typically in reference to military manoeuvres since the early 1800s. The derivative noun *débouché* can ultimately be used to refer to any opening, outlet, or exit where 'debouching' can take place – or, figuratively, a gap in the market for selling a new product.

### *Emeute*

Derived from verb *émouvoir* meaning 'to agitate' or 'to move'. In French an *émeute* is a riot, or chaos or disruption It has been used in English to refer to a social uprising or disturbance since the late 1700s.

# 10 - Literature and Drama

## *Genre*

French word dating from 1770 and used to describe a particular type of art or literature. It was introduced into English from c.1840s.

## *Jusqu'auboutisme*

In French, *jusqu'au bout* means 'to the limit' or 'to the very end'. The term *jusqu'auboutisme* emerged in France during the First World War to refer to a policy of absolute unwavering perseverance, of continuing to fight until the bitter end, or when a full and lasting conclusion to the conflict could finally be reached.

The term first appeared in English in that context in a newspaper report in 1917, but its meaning has steadily broadened and weakened since then. Nowadays, *jusqu'auboutisme* refers to any dogged determination to see something through to its final conclusion.

## *Nouveau Riche*

A French phrase, literally meaning 'new rich', 'one who has recently acquired wealth; a wealthy upstart'.

In English literature, it means 'a person who has recently acquired wealth and is regarded as vulgarly ostentatious or lacking in social graces' (Merriam-Webster dictionary).

## *Plaisanteur*

A derivative of a French verb meaning 'to jest' or 'quip'. A *plaisanteur* is a witty talker or storyteller. The word *plaisantin* is used in French nowadays.

### *Pudeur*

From the French word *pudeur* and from Latin *pudeo*: 'I am ashamed'.

Borrowed into English in the late 19th century, *pudeur* means 'bashfulness or reticence', or else 'a feeling of shame or embarrassment'.

### *Douceur*

From the French 17th century word, a *douceur* is a small gift or payment, sometimes, but not necessarily, considered a bribe, provided by someone to enhance or sweeten a deal.

It is no longer used in this sense in modern French.

### *Ménage*

From the French word *ménage* which is from the Old French word *manage* meaning 'household, family dwelling' (12th century), and also from the Vulgar Latin word *mansionaticum meaning* 'household, that which pertains to a house', which is derived from the Latin *mansionem meaning* 'dwelling'.

Nowadays it is generally used in the suggestive borrowed French phrase *ménage à trois* meaning 'a domestic arrangement or relationship consisting of a husband, a wife, and the lover of one or the other', literally 'household of three'.

## Theatre and Drama

When looking into the influence of the French language on British theatre there are a number of examples of vocabulary with French roots. In some cases the word is exactly the same while in others the word has been anglicised.

## *Décor*

In the 14th century. the verb *décorer* (Latin root) meant to decorate, adorn or beautify and by the 19th century the term 'décor' was used in Britain to refer to stage sets. In the 20th century the use of the word 'décor' was expanded to include home decoration.

## *Comedy*

The 14th century Old French word *comédie* meant a poem. By the mid 16th century the word 'comedy' was used in theatre here to denote a comic play or drama and by the later years of the 19th century. it was also used in a more general way to describe an amusing event or situation.

## *Costume*

*Costume* in 17th-century France meant fashion or habit and then style of dress. The term was used in theatre in this country to refer to customary clothes of the particular period in which a scene is set. It is still used in this way today but has also passed into more general use.

## *Hero*

Originally the word *heroe* (Greek root) in Old French was used to describe someone of superhuman strength. By the 1660s the word was in use here to denote a man who exhibited great bravery. From the 1690s onwards the word 'hero' took on an additional meaning, that of a chief male character.

### Intrigue

The French use of the word *intrigue* dates back to the 14th century meaning to deceive, trick or cheat. By the 17th century intrigue as used here carried connotations of clandestine or illicit sexual relationships. By the 18th century it was recorded as having a more general meaning: to plot or scheme.

### Mime

In ancient literature mimes were dramatic performances with spoken lines but by the $16^{th}$ century. the French word *mime* meant 'mimic actor'. In 1600 Dr. Johnson records its use in English as a 'buffoon who practices gesticulation'.

### Scene

The 14th-century French word *scène* has its roots in Latin and Greek and means 'scene', or stage of the theatre. It was recorded as meaning the place in which action takes place in the 1590s in England.

### Tragedy

*Tragédie* (Latin and Greek roots) in Old French was a term for a dramatic work with an unhappy ending. While it is still used in that way today it was also used to describe any unhappy event or disaster from around 1500.

## Conclusion

Try as some might to break the links and liaisons with the French, the language forms a rich part of English literature, drama theatre and art and will remain so. The use of French in literature enhances, enriches, endows and elevates the language to a stature wherein ideas and thoughts are more adeptly expressed and explored. Unless the linguistic borders are closed and migrant words sent back to their origin there will never be 'sovereignty' over the English language. The world is now too mobile and fluid, and too interconnected to allow for isolationism.

# 10 - Literature and Drama

## References

Eells, Emily (2013) 'L'étranger dans la langue' in: Berthin. C. and Déprats, J-M. *Chemins croisés.* Presses universitaires de Paris Ouest.

Jerdan, William (1838), 'The Windsor Ball of the Latest Fashion', in Richard Bentley (ed.) *Bentley's Miscellany* (Volume 3). London: Richard Bentley.

Mental Floss (2017) *30 Little-Used Loanwords To Add Some Je Ne Sais Quoi To Your Vocabulary* [online]. Available at: <https://www.mentalfloss.com/article/91652/30-little-used-loanwords-add-some-je-ne-sais-quoi-your-vocabulary> [Accessed 3 Nov. 2021].

Merriam-Webster (n.d.) *Nouveau riche* in Merriam-Webster.com thesaurus. Retrieved November 3, 2021, from https://www.merriam-webster.com/thesaurus/nouveau%20riche.

This chapter uses material from the following Wikipedia articles, which are released under the <https://creativecommons.org/licenses/by-sa/3.0/> Creative Commons Attribution-Share-Alike License 3.0.

<https://en.wikipedia.org/wiki/Influence_of_French_on_English>

<https://en.wikipedia.org/wiki/S%C3%A9ance>[Accessed 10 November 2021].

# 10 - Literature and Drama

# 10 - Literature and Drama

# Acknowledgements

This book would never have seen the light of day without a lot of help and advice from many people. In particular, Clandon French gratefully acknowledges Sally Daniells, Danielle Frank, Catherine Morelle, Guy Morelle and Linda Morelle who generously gave up their time to read the manuscript and offer invaluable advice which improved the book enormously. In spite of all the support received and many sources consulted, some errors are bound to remain. These are entirely due to the authors.

# Acknowledgements

# Index

# Index

# Index

# Index

# Index

# Index

# Index

# About the Authors

Clandon French is the *nom de plume* of a small group who meet regularly to talk in French. The members of the group come from different backgrounds but are bound together by their love of the French language. The meetings are an opportunity to enthusiastically discuss a wide range of topics ranging from current affairs to fashion, always with a nod to the similarities and differences between the English and French languages and culture. The group has had to meet virtually since the start of the Covid-19 pandemic and this book arose out of virtual discussions about whether French words commonly used in English would be understood in the same way by French people.

Printed in Great Britain
by Amazon